CITYSPOTS
LYON

G000139696

WHAT'S IN YOUR GUIDEBOOK?

Independent authors Impartial up-to-date information from our travel experts who meticulously source local knowledge.

Experience Thomas Cook's 165 years in the travel industry and guidebook publishing enriches every word with expertise you can trust.

Travel know-how Contributions by thousands of staff around the globe, each one living and breathing travel.

Editors Travel-publishing professionals, pulling everything together to craft a perfect blend of words, pictures, maps and design.

You, the traveller We deliver a practical, no-nonsense approach to information, geared to how you really use it.

CITYSPOTS
LYON

Anwer Bati

Written by Anwer Bati
Original photography by Anwer Bati
Cover photo (Opéra du Lyon) © Cozzi Guido / www.4cornersimages.com
Series design based on an original concept by Studio 183 Limited

Produced by Cambridge Publishing Management Limited
Project Editor: Amanda Learmonth
Layout: Trevor Double
Maps: PC Graphics
Transport map: © Communicarta Limited

Published by Thomas Cook Publishing
A division of Thomas Cook Tour Operations Limited
Company Registration No. 1450464 England
PO Box 227, Unit 18, Coningsby Road
Peterborough PE3 8SB, United Kingdom
email: books@thomascook.com
www.thomascookpublishing.com
+ 44 (0) 1733 416477
ISBN: 978-1-84157-765-4

First edition © 2007 Thomas Cook Publishing
Text © 2007 Thomas Cook Publishing
Maps © 2007 Thomas Cook Publishing
Series/Project Editor: Kelly Anne Pipes
Production/DTP: Steven Collins

Printed and bound in Spain by GraphyCems

CONTENTS

SYMBOLS KEY

The following symbols are used throughout this book:

ⓐ address   ⓣ telephone   ⓦ website address
ⓞ opening times   ⓝ public transport connections   ⓘ important

The following symbols are used on the maps:

𝒊	information office	O	city
✈	airport	O	large town
➕	hospital	○	small town
Ⓤ	police station	=	motorway
🚌	bus station	—	main road
🚆	railway station	—	minor road
Ⓜ	metro	—	railway
✝	cathedral		
➊	numbers denote featured cafés & restaurants		

Hotels and restaurants are graded by approximate price
as follows:
£ budget   ££ mid-range   £££ expensive

◗ *The Cathédrale St-Jean and Basilique Notre-Dame*

INTRODUCING
Lyon

Introduction

Lyon (sometimes spelt Lyons in English) is the capital of the Rhône department, in east-central France, spread over an area between the Rhône and Saône rivers. Even though it is the third largest city in France, it is second (to Paris) in the size of its economy: particularly focused on textiles and chemicals, as well as manufacturing. So it is a major business and industrial city, as well as being an important destination for visitors, who are attracted by its culture and lifestyle. Lyon also has a large university (the most important outside Paris), spread over three campuses, and many young people live there as a result.

The city is steeped in a history that stretches back to Roman times, with a Roman theatre and amphitheatre. Vieux Lyon (the Old Town) is one of the finest Renaissance sites of its type. But it is also a vibrant modern city, with some fine contemporary architecture, and major cultural attractions – in terms of both art and performance. Lyon is perhaps the most important centre of gastronomy in France, and the home of some of the finest chefs in the country. So food and drink are taken very seriously, and attract many visitors. It is well served by the transport system, with an underground railway opened in 1978, and a TGV station (in the Part-Dieu suburb) opened two years later. Because of its location it is also a very good base for excursions – particularly to Provence in the south, and the Beaujolais and Burgundy vineyards to the north.

Lyon is divided into several distinct areas, old and new. It has the attractions and amenities of a major city, as well as its considerable historical heritage. On the whole, people who visit go for the food and the culture, though there are also plenty of other activities on offer.

🔺 Wander through the charming cobbled streets of Vieux Lyon

When to go

CLIMATE

Winters in Lyon are cool, but rarely very cold (there are only a couple of days of snow a year), though it can be foggy with some rain. Spring and autumn are pleasant and mild, with the average maximum temperature reaching as high as 21°C (70°F), though April and October are among the rainiest months. Summers are hot and dry, but can be somewhat muggy, with air quality affected by local chemical works. The average maximum temperature in August is 27°C (81°F). Summer evenings tend to be warm. On the whole though, spring and autumn are the best times to visit, particularly if you intend to do a lot of sightseeing.

ANNUAL EVENTS

Lyon has major cultural, sporting and trade events throughout the year. Apart from those listed below, there are also many performances. Check the Lyon tourist office ⓣ 04 72 77 69 69 ⓦ www.lyon-france.com for further details.

January
Salon Sirha and Bocuse d'Or is a catering, food and hotel trade show, held on alternate, odd-numbered, years.
ⓦ www.sirha.com
Voyage Musical d'Hiver ('Winter Journey' chamber music festival) third week in Jan. Contact Salle Molière
ⓐ 20 quai de Bondy ⓣ 04 72 10 38 23

March–April

Musicades (Chamber music festival) ☎ reservations 04 72 20 02 88 ⓦ www.musicades.com

Lyon-Charbonnières Car Rally ⓦ www.asarhone.com

Lyon Marathon ⓦ www.marathondelyon.com

Saint-Georges Carnival ⓦ www.dragons.st.georges.online.fr

May

Festival Les Nuits Sonores (Sound Nights Festival) electronic music performed by top artists. ⓦ www.nuits-sonores.com

Festival les Intranquilles (Literature festival) ☎ information and booking 04 78 39 10 02 ⓦ www.lesintranquilles.net

🔵 *Place Bellecour makes for a popular meeting place*

June–July

Le Festival de Théâtre Jeune Public (Theatre Festival for Young People) June, alternate, odd-numbered, years. ⓦ www.biennle-tja.fr

Festival du Cinéma Nouvelle Génération Film festival featuring inventive work by young directors (June).
ⓦ www.cinemanouvellegeneration.com

Nuits de Fourvière Six weeks of concert, theatre and dance performances in the old Roman theatre. ⓣ 04 72 57 15 40
ⓦ www.nuits-de-fourviere.org

Le quai des Guingettes Open-air cafés, music and dancing by the river (three days in mid-July).

August

Tout l'Monde Dehors Free outdoor events and performances around the city.

September

Biennale International de Danse (International Dance Biennial) alternate, even-numbered, years. ⓦ www.biennale-de-lyon.org

Biennale d'Art Contemporain (Contemporary Art Biennial) alternate, odd-numbered, years. Both the Biennales have been going since 1991, and are major events. ⓦ www.biennale-de-lyon.org

Vieux-Lyon Tupiniers Pottery market, second weekend, in place St-Jean

October

Tennis Grand Prix (see page 35)

Salon de Automobile (Car Show) held on alternate, odd-numbered, years. ⓣ 04 72 22 33 44 ⓦ www.salonautolyon.com

November–December

Sortie du Beaujolais Nouveau (Arrival of Beaujolais Nouveau) Held on the third Thur in Nov.

Festival de Musique Ancienne (Ancient Music Festival) Held from late Nov–mid-Dec in the baroque splendour of the Chapel of the Trinity. Ⓦ www.lachapelle-lyon.org

Fête des Lumières (Festival of Lights) Held 7–10 Dec (see page 14).

Christmas Market On place Carnot, near Perrache station.

PUBLIC HOLIDAYS

Public transport runs to Sunday schedules, and banks, post offices and public buildings are closed. Many shops (but usually not restaurants) will also be closed. Some museums may also close or change their admission times.

New Year's Day 1 January

Easter (Pâques) Late March/early April

Labour Day (Fête du Travail) 1 May

Victory Day (World War II) 8 May

Ascension Day (40 days after Easter) May

Whit Sunday and Monday (seventh Sun after Easter) May/June

Bastille Day 14 July

Assumption (Assomption) 15 August

All Saints' Day (Toussaint) 1 November

Armistice Day 11 November

Christmas Day (Noël) 25 December

The Festival of Lights

The tradition of a festival of light extends back to 1852 when the old bell tower of the former Fourvière chapel was reconstructed, and a statue of the Virgin Mary was supposed to be placed on top. The date was fixed for 8 September but work wasn't completed in time, so the ceremony was postponed to the day of the Fête of the Immaculate Conception on 8 December, with a programme of festivities and illuminations planned that night. But heavy rain fell throughout the day, and the church authorities decided to postpone the celebrations once again. The rain ceased by the evening and the Lyonnais (particularly those in the Fourvière district) celebrated by spontaneously placing candles in their windows and on their balconies – a tradition followed to this day.

As a result of this tradition, in 1989 Lyon became one of the first cities in France to institute a plan for public lighting as a deliberate policy to highlight the city's architecture. This led to the emergence of a group of creative lighting designers, such as Alain Guilhot, Roland Jéol and Pierre Marcout. Light is now used throughout Lyon at night to enhance the city's monuments, public buildings, and the contours of the rivers it lies between. In fact, Lyon is now one of the world's leading cities in its use of public lighting – so much so that the electronics firm Philips actually set up its European head office for exterior lighting near the city in 1996.

Since 2000, Lyon has taken this reputation further by instigating its famous Festival of Lights (around 8 December for four nights), during which artists and lighting designers transform the city with an array of coloured illuminations and projections. The dazzling and varied displays around town mean that the streets of Lyon throng with hundreds of thousands of people – both locals and visitors.

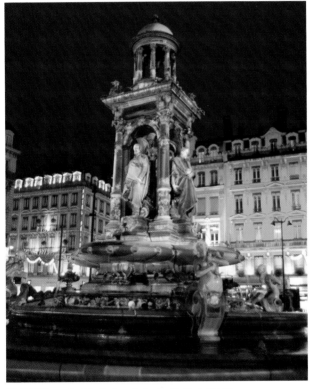

● *Lyon becomes a riot of colour during the Festival of Lights*

History

Founded on the banks of the Rhône and Saône rivers, Lyon was originally a Celtic settlement. It became a Roman colony, named Lugdunum in 43 BC, becoming capital of Gaul in 1 BC and a major trade centre. The Romans built on both the Fourvière and Croix-Rousse hills, and the architectural evidence of their presence can still be seen today.

The city also became a centre of Christianity. But the population moved from Fourvière to settle along the Saône and in the St-Jean area as a result of barbarian invasions. The medieval period saw much of the population leaving the crowded St-Jean area and moving to the peninsula (the Presqu'île area). It was also a period of intensive building, including the abbey of St-Martin d'Ainay. But the increasingly prosperous merchants and bankers also wanted more independence from the power of the Church. They appealed to the kingdom of France, and the city became part of France in 1312.

The Hundred Years' War and the Black Death in the 14th and 15th centuries led to a decline in the city's prosperity but it was flourishing again by the middle of the 15th century – with wealthy merchants, many of them Italian, moving to what is now Vieux Lyon (the Old Town).

In 1528 François I granted local weavers the right to make cloth using gold and silver, and the silk industry, for which Lyon became so notable, came into being. Soon, Lyon became renowned across Europe for its textiles, and France's first stock exchange opened here in 1506. Lyon also became a centre for printing and literature including the presence, for a time, of Rabelais.

The Wars of Religion – the conflict between Catholics and Protestants – took their toll on the city during the 16th century, with several massacres. By the 17th century, however, there was considerable urban development, and the city centre moved to Presqu'île. By the time of the French Revolution, Lyon was the most important economic centre in France, but the upheavals of the Revolution led to the collapse of the silk industry. Many of its citizens were also killed, and parts of the city destroyed, including the many religious institutions on Fourvière Hill.

The textile industry was back on its feet by the early 19th century, however, and Lyon embraced the Industrial Revolution, expanding considerably in the next 100 years. The chemical and pharmaceutical industries also grew – partly as a result of research into dyes and new fabrics. The very first film was shown in Lyon in 1895.

Lyon, as a centre of the French Resistance, suffered in World War II, but from the 1950s onwards underwent further expansion and modernisation. The G7 summit of world leaders was held here in 1996. Lyon also houses the headquarters of Interpol. Today greater Lyon has a population of over 2 million (though the city centre houses around 500,000 people). Vieux Lyon, and the surrounding area, was put on UNESCO's World Heritage List in 1998.

Lifestyle

With its commercial history, it's hardly surprising that Lyon is a largely bourgeois city, where business, family, culture and a strong work ethic are central to life. But it is also on the fringes of the south of France, and life is somewhat more relaxed than in cities further north. With excellent transport links, many Lyonnais think nothing of visiting the bordering Beaujolais and Rhône vineyards, the Alps or going south for the weekend. And, because wine and gastronomy are such a feature of life, they are very discerning about eating and drinking, and basically like to enjoy themselves when not working – though you will see few people on the streets after 22.00, except at weekends.

The Lyonnais have a reputation for being polite but reserved – keeping the secrets of their city to themselves – but this is changing, particularly since more visitors started coming to the city after its UNESCO nomination. Even so, some 70 per cent of visitors come for business, rather than tourism. Because of its history of business – and the many trade fairs held here – the Lyonnais display none of the cynicism of more obvious tourist cities further south. And a fair number of people speak English, particularly in hotels and restaurants. Since it is not primarily a tourist city, prices are generally reasonable.

The Lyonnais take considerable pride in their city and its history – as well as its contemporary achievements – and expect visitors to do the same. And rowdy, disrespectful or drunken behaviour is seriously frowned upon. The people of Lyon also enjoy the architecture, public spaces, parks, walks and river banks of their city. They're also proud of their infrastructure –

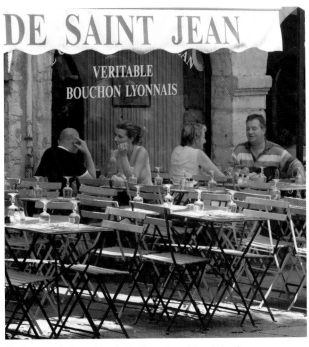

with its notably good public transport system – and a quality of life that's generally better than in any other major city in France. Add to that the fact that the cultural life of the city is second only to that of Paris, with major international performers appearing regularly and top quality sporting events and festivals, and you can understand the Lyonnais are a pretty contented lot.

DE SAINT JEAN

VERITABLE
BOUCHON LYONNAIS

The Lyonnais like nothing better than a long, leisurely lunch

Culture

After Paris, Lyon is the leading cultural centre in France. It has major museums, theatres, private galleries, and world-class events and performances.

The main art museums include the Musée des Beaux-Arts (see page 81) in the Presqu'île area, with a fine collection of old masters, and the best collection of Impressionists in France, other than the Musée d'Orsay in Paris. The Cité International area on the left bank of the Rhône houses the Musée d'Art Contemporain (ⓦ www.moca.lyon.org), the contemporary art museum that is also an important site during Lyon's famous art biennial. You will also find large murals around Lyon, illustrating its history. Several of these decorate the museum dedicated to the innovative 19th and early 20th-century local architect Tony Garnier.

The city's long and rich history is also reflected in many of its museums and sights. These include the Roman theatre (see page 71) and Musée de la Civilisation Gallo-Romaine (see page 69) on Fourvière Hill and the amphitheatre of Croix-Rousse (see page 94); and fine houses, among them the Musée Gadagne (see page 69) in Vieux Lyon (with a museum evoking Lyon's history). Lyon's importance as a centre of silk production means that there is also a textile museum (Musée des Tissus) (see page 83); and its skill in decorative arts is celebrated in the Musée des Arts Décoratifs (see page 83). Lyon's sombre experience of World War II is commemorated in the Centre d'Histoire de la Résistance et de la Déportation (the Resistance and Deportation History Centre) (ⓣ 04 78 72 23 11).

Music is an important part of local cultural life, with major concerts and festivals around the city throughout the year, often attracting leading international talent. And dance, too, particularly the prestigious dance biennial, is an important feature. The Maison de la Dance is the city's leading venue. Lyon's opera house, reconstructed by celebrated architect

🔺 *The graceful cloisters of the Musée des Beaux-Arts*

Jean Nouvel (only the façade is now left of the original building), is the most important outside Paris, with often dazzling productions. It houses both an orchestra and a resident ballet company. There is also a resident orchestra at the Auditorium and the city has several theatres.

Cinema was invented in Lyon by the Lumière brothers, and it's therefore not surprising that Lyon hosts many film events, including outdoor screenings from June–September. The Institut Lumière (ⓦ www.institut-lumiere.org) is dedicated to the early history of moving pictures.

Lyon's architecture is a major cultural attraction. There are medieval and Renaissance buildings in Vieux Lyon, the 18th- and 19th-century buildings of Presqu'île, and the modern developments on the east bank of the Rhône, including architect Renzo Piano's Cité Internationale.

LYON CITY CARD

It's well worth getting the Lyon City Card. Not only does it give you unlimited travel on Lyon's bus and underground system (tickets are included in the wallet), but also admission to 19 museums, as well as other concessions including admission to various events. You can buy it at the tourist office, TCL public transport offices, and at many larger hotels. It's €18 for one day, €28 for two days and €38 for three days. The card is half-price for visitors under 18.

◗ A colourful array of silk fabrics for sale

Shopping

Lyon offers some of the best, most varied and most interesting shopping in France. Given the city's history of silk and textile design and manufacture, it's not surprising that fashion and fabrics feature high on the list of shopping attractions. The most famous Lyon designers include Nathalie Chaize, Max Chaoul, Korloff, Jean-Claude Trigon and Marie Michaud. What's known as the Carré d'Or (between place Bellecour and Cordeliers) is full of major designer shops, as well as some upmarket foodstores. The 19th-century passage de l'Argue (between the rue de la République and rue Edouard Herriot) is an arcade with small fashion and upmarket craft shops. The pedestrianised area, one of the biggest in Europe, in Presqu'île (around rue Victor Hugo and rue de la République) is where you will find major international chains. And the shopping centre in the Part-Dieu area (near the TGV station) has more than 200 shops, including department stores such as Galeries Lafayette.

The rue Auguste Compte, to the south of Bellecour, is the place to go for antiques, art, jewellery, fabric and interiors shops. The passage Thiaffait in Croix-Rousse is an arcade with small local designer boutiques and other attractive shops. In Vieux Lyon, traditional arts and crafts shops mingle with more touristy outlets.

For food, make your way (the no. 1 bus goes there) to the new covered Halles on the east bank of the Rhône and the old Halles in rue de la Marinière. You should also head for the markets along boulevard de la Croix-Rousse, and the lively food and flower market on quai St-Antoine on the banks of the Saône,

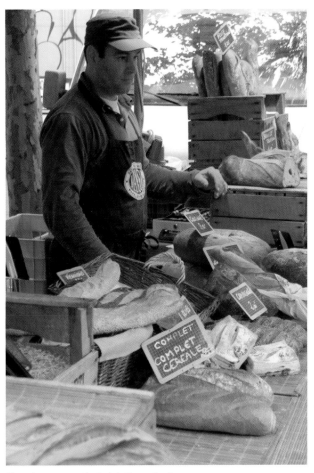

🔺 Boulangeries *can be found all over the city*

though you will also find several other smaller ones. There is a craft market (Sun morning) on the quai Rolland. Most markets open early morning, and close at 13.00, though many stall holders start packing up somewhat earlier. If you want to buy wine, it's best to go to a specialist wine shop or a supermarket – unless you choose to go on a tour to one of the local vineyards, in which case you can buy direct.

USEFUL SHOPPING PHRASES

How much is this?
C'est combien?
Cey combyahng?

Can I try this on?
Puis-je essayer ceci?
Pweezh ehssayeh cerssee?

My size is...
Ma taille (clothes)/
ma pointure (shoes) est ...
Mah tie/mah
pooahngtewr ay ...

I'll take this one, thank you
Je prends celui-ci/
celle-ci merci
Zher prahng serlweesi/
Mah sehlsee mehrsee

Eating & drinking

Lyon is one of the greatest foodie destinations in France, with many fine gastronomic restaurants, as well as some more modest, but good, establishments. Because it is the main city in the large Rhône-Alpes region, renowned for the quality of its produce, Lyon's chefs have easy access to some of the finest ingredients in France. Indeed, they make the most of them. Chefs maintain a strong feeling for tradition as well as being inspired to be creative. Lyonnais cuisine tends to be on the hearty side, but many younger chefs are now cooking light, modern food, with the odd foreign influence.

Outside of Paris, Lyon and its surrounding area has more Michelin-starred chefs than any other part of France. This starlight started shining with Fernand Point, who was the first chef to be awarded three Michelin stars, in 1933 at La Pyramide (see page 125) in nearby Vienne. Later came local culinary hero Paul Bocuse. Today's big names still include Bocuse, but also Lacombe, Orsi, Chavent, and a new generation such as Nicolas le Bec, Christian Têteodoie, Sonia Ezsgulian and Philippe Gauvreau.

Apart from its gastronomic restaurants, brasseries and cafés, Lyon is also famous for its *bouchons* – small restaurants, often family-run, serving relatively simple and traditional food. The

RESTAURANT PRICE CATEGORIES
Average price for a three-course meal (without drinks).
A lunch or a set menu will often be cheaper.
£ = €20 or under   ££ = €20–60   £££ = over €60

original *bouchons*, of which only a handful survive, at the foot of Croix-Rousse (see page 101), were inns that served coachmen drinks and snacks while their horses were being brushed down (*bouchonner*).

Meat is the mainstay of the Lyonnais menu, but local dishes cover a very wide range. Specialities such as sausages (including *andouillette*, the chitterling sausage; and *cervelas truffé* – truffled saveloy). Tripe and other forms of offal are also local favourites (*tablier de sapeur* – breaded tripe, for instance), as is *quenelles de brochet* (pike dumplings).

Onions are widely used in cooking, as in calf's liver *à la lyonnaise*. *Galettes lyonnais* are pancakes made with potatoes and onions. *Gratin dauphinois* is the best known potato dish of the region, baked with milk or cream and garlic. Desserts include *tarte à la lyonnaise*, with almonds. Waffles (*gauffres*) are also popular and chestnuts (*marrons*) are a feature of many desserts and other dishes. Cheeses from the region include

◔ *Sausages are a local speciality*

Picadon, St-Marcellin (the most popular), Tomme de Savoie, Reblochon, Comté and Rigotte.

Although most Lyonnais prefer to have a leisurely meal, you should have no difficulty in finding crêperies and pizzerias; bakeries (*boulangeries*) and pâtisseries where you can find snacks such as mini-pizzas and pastries; and delicatessens where you can buy food for picnicking along the river banks or in one of the city's many green spaces. Lyon also has many food markets (see page 24).

THE REGION'S WINES

The local joke is that three rivers run through Lyon: the Rhône, the Saône and Beaujolais. And since Lyon is very near the vineyards of Beaujolais and the northern Rhône valley (Côte du Rhône wines), it's unlikely that you will be served a bad glass of wine, particularly if it's red. The most famous Beaujolais wines include Brouilly, Morgon and Fleurie. Among the best of the Côte du Rhônes are Côte Rôtie, Hermitage and Saint Joseph. Coteaux du Lyonnais wines from west of Lyon consist of fruity reds, whites and rosés. You will also come across many other good wines from the Rhône-Alpes region, including Condrieu, du Bugey, du Varais and Côtes du Forez. The cheapest wines are usually served in *pots* – 46 or 50 cl bottles, rather than carafes, as in other parts of France. There are also many liqueurs from the region made from fruits and nuts. The most famous of these is green or (sweeter) yellow Chartreuse, made with herbs.

Most restaurants open from 12.00–14.00 or 14.30, and then from 19.00 or 19.30–21.30 or 22.00. Most Lyonnais eat dinner at around 20.00. Simpler brasseries and cafés open much earlier, and close later. They are usually open all day, though many serve food only during dining hours. Some restaurants close for a couple of weeks each year, often in August or winter: so always check, particularly if you want to visit an upmarket establishment.

Service is included in French restaurants and bars. So there is no need to leave a tip.

At the time of writing, most restaurants and cafés have separate smoking and non-smoking areas. However, new laws are going to be introduced for restaurants, bars and clubs from early 2008, banning indoor smoking.

USEFUL DINING PHRASES

I would like a table for ... people

Je voudrais une table pour ... personnes

Zher voodray ewn tabl poor ... pehrson

May I have the bill, please?

L'addition, s'il vous plaît!

Laddyssyawng, sylvooplay!

Waiter/waitress!

Monsieur/Mademoiselle, s'il vous plaît?

M'sewr/madmwahzel, sylvooplay!

Does it have meat in it?

Est-ce que ce plat contient de la viande?

Essker ser plah kontyang der lah veeahngd?

Where is the toilet please?

Où sont les toilettes, s'il vous plaît?

Oo sawng leh twahlaitt, sylvooplay?

Entertainment & nightlife

With a large student population and many cultural venues, Lyon does better than most French provincial cities for entertainment and nightlife. For a start, there are many performances by leading international musicians and singers, whether classical or current, including rock concerts. Productions at the Opera House are of the highest quality, and apart from the Théâtre des Célestins, with its classical productions, there are several other theatres in Lyon, including the Théâtre des Ateliers in Presqu'île and the Théâtre de la Croix-Rousse. But plays are in French, of course.

The Roman theatre at Fourvière comes into its own with open-air concerts, dance and other performances during the Nuits de Fourvière (see page 12). There are also open-air events at night during Lyon's many other festivals, including films from June–September in the Roman theatre and the town's squares. Dance performances of all types are another attraction – and there is no language barrier.

Apart from bars and cafés, some of which stay open until 01.00, or later, there are also a number of discos and nightclubs in Lyon. You'll find most happening in the evening in Presqu'île, and in Vieux Lyon, but also on the east bank of the Rhône, particularly in the lively area in and around the old Brotteaux railway station. But don't expect a lot of action during the week: Fridays and Saturdays are when the Lyonnais stay out late.

Don't forget that walking along the river banks, particularly of the Saône, is a major attraction after dark.

○ *The splendid Théâtre des Célestins stages classical productions*

Go to the tourist office website ⓦ www.lyon-france.com for event and performance listings and ticket details. Also check ⓦ www.lyon.fr. *Lyon City News* (in both English and French) is also published by the tourist office, and contains a lot of useful information about what's on, and where to go. *Le Petit Paumé* (if you can get hold of a copy: it's only distributed once a year) has very comprehensive listings of bars and restaurants, and is free, or try its website ⓦ www.petitpaume.com. Both the book and the website are in French. Also in French is the weekly listings magazine *Lyon Poche*.

CINEMATIC HERITAGE

As the birthplace of films, Lyon has around ten cinemas in the World Heritage area, mostly in Presqu'île. The Institut Lumière, a museum that traces the early history of moving pictures with interesting exhibits and videos, has cinema seasons based around directors or themes – go to ⓦ www.institut-lumiere.org. French cinemas normally show dubbed versions of mainstream foreign films, though art house films are often shown in their original languages (including English) and are subtitled. There are around a dozen movie events during the year.

○ *Lyon's streets come alive on weekend nights*

Sport & relaxation

Lyon has all the normal sporting facilities and relaxation possibilities you would expect from a large city. Apart from walking or cycling (see page 55) around town, you will also find swimming pools including the outdoor Centre Nautique du Rhône, just on the east bank of the river, opposite the main post office. ⓐ quai Bernard ⓣ 04 78 72 04 50. Several of the bigger hotels also have pools. Check with ⓦ www.lyon.fr for the one nearest to where you're staying. The website is in English as well as French. There are also several gyms and public tennis facilities around town. Check on the same website.

For spectator sports, there is the Tennis Grand Prix in October. ⓐ Palais des Sports, 350 av Jean Jaurès ⓣ 04 72 22 25 63 ⓦ www.gptennislyon.com for ticket details or book on ⓦ www.progrescope.com

The other main sports to watch are the leading ASVEL basketball team in the suburb of Villeurbanne ⓐ 451 cours Emile Zola ⓣ 04 72 14 17 13 ⓦ www.asvel.com. And of course, football, with Olympique Lyonnais, several times French champions, and a team including international stars. ⓐ Stade Garland, 350 av Jean Jaurès ⓣ 04 72 76 76 04 ⓦ www.olweb.fr

Spa days

If you really want to relax, there are spas dotted around Lyon, including:

Lyon Plage – the largest urban spa in Europe at the Métropole hotel, on the banks of the Saône. ⓐ 85 quai Joseph Gillet ⓣ 04 72 10 44 44 ⓦ www.lyon-plage.com

Royal Spa – on the east bank of the Rhône. ⓐ 75 cours Vitton
ⓣ 04 78 89 97 74 ⓦ www.royalspa.fr

Cruises

If you just want to have an easy time, you can always take a
cruise along the Saône during the day or evening, and have
lunch or dinner on board. There are several possibilities (check
with the tourist office) but try:

Bateau City de Lyon ⓐ quai des Célestins ⓣ 06 25 92 25 69
ⓦ www.bateauvolupte.com ⓛ Apr–Oct

Navig'inter, leaving from 16 quai Bernard. ⓐ 13 bis quai
Rambaud ⓣ 04 78 42 96 81 ⓦ www.naviginter.fr ⓛ closed Feb

▲ Bicycles are perfect for a sightseeing trip around Lyon

Accommodation

Lyon has all types of accommodation, though much of it is outside the UNESCO World Heritage area. But note that hotel accommodation is in short supply during the city's many business events and conferences. So make sure you book well in advance. New hotels are being built, but prices are relatively high for a French provincial city. Many hotels include a buffet breakfast in their rates; others charge a hefty supplement.

Unless you have booked an inclusive package, it pays to investigate thoroughly on the web. The Lyon tourist website (ⓦ www.lyon-france.com) carries a comprehensive list of hotels, their facilities and locations, and you can book online. It also provides links to the hotels' own websites. Unlike many destinations, weekends tend to be easier to book, as there are fewer business events. Listed below are some recommendations, but there are many more good hotels to choose from. The ratings indicate average price per double room per night. Some rooms, particularly those with or without views, may be more or less expensive than the ratings suggest.

Hotels

Bayard £ Small, simple and rather offbeat, but well located.
ⓐ 23 pl Bellecour ⓣ 04 78 37 39 64 ⓦ www.hotelbayard.com
ⓝ Metro: Bellecour

Foch £ A charming and well-appointed hotel, with good services and a restaurant. Located on the east bank of the Rhône, in the Brotteaux district, not far from the Cité Internationale.

PRICE RATING
Average price for a room for two:
£ = under €100   ££ = €100–200   £££ = over €200

🅐 59 av. de Maréchal Foch 🅣 04 78 89 14 01 🅦 www.hotel-foch.fr
🅝 Metro: Foch

Des Artistes £–££ Bright, pleasant and comfortable, by the
pl des Célestins. 🅐 8 rue Gaspard André 🅣 04 78 42 04 88
🅦 www.hoteldesartistes.fr 🅝 Metro: Bellecour

Collège ££ A very unusual hotel, where the rooms are all white
and the place is decorated with items – such as desks, lockers
and textbooks – used in French schools in the 1950s and 60s.
There are several other retro items, including early 60s fridges
on each floor with free soft drinks. The bar/breakfast room is
decked out like a classroom. 🅐 5 pl St-Paul 🅣 04 72 10 05 05
🅦 www.college-hotel.com 🅝 Metro: Vieux Lyon

Globe et Cécil ££ A good choice, with 60 elegantly decorated
rooms (no two rooms are the same) in a hotel that's more than
a century old. 🅐 21 rue Gasparin 🅣 04 78 42 58 95
🅦 www.globeetcecilhotel.com 🅝 Metro: Bellecour

Mercure Lyon Beaux-Arts ££ A very comfortable business hotel,
run by the Mercure chain, so pretty reliable. 🅐 74 rue Edouard
Herriot 🅣 04 78 38 09 50 🅦 www.mercure.com
🅝 Metro: Bellecour

⬥ The Collège hotel offers a unique, retro experience

Roosevelt ££ A cosy place with a good bar, close to Tête d'Or park and Part-Dieu station. ⓐ 48 rue de Sèze ⓣ 04 78 52 35 67 ⓦ www.hotel-roosevelt.com ⓜ Metro: Masséna

Cour des Loges £££ Built around a courtyard, and housed in four buildings dating from the 14th, 16th and 17th centuries, this very stylish hotel has modern rooms, a good restaurant, a pool and

● *The stylish lobby of Villa Florentine provides a warm welcome*

an atmospheric bar. ⓐ 6 rue du Boeuf ❶ 04 72 77 44 44
Ⓦ www.courdesloges.com Ⓝ Metro: Vieux Lyon

La Tour Rose £££ With 12 suites decorated in silk, in homage to
the local textile industry, and housed in three buildings dating
from the 15th to the 18th centuries. This is one of Lyon's most
extraordinary hotels, with two good restaurants and a
charming, if somewhat eccentric, owner, Jacques Champion.
ⓐ 22 rue du Boeuf ❶ 04 78 92 69 10 Ⓦ www.tour-rose.com
Ⓝ Metro: Vieux Lyon

Villa Florentine £££ Recognised as the best hotel in Lyon, with
wonderful views from the exceptionally comfortable rooms, and
the large pool. It was once a convent, and couldn't be better
placed for Vieux Lyon and Fourvière (it's on the lower part of the
hill). It also boasts one of the best restaurants in town (see page
74) and private parking. ⓐ 25 montée Saint-Barthélemy ❶ 04 72
56 56 56 Ⓦ www.villaflorentine.com Ⓝ Metro: Vieux Lyon

Bed & breakfasts
For B&Bs you could contact the tourist office website Ⓦ www.
bb-lyon.com (you can get a double room with breakfast from
€34–53 per night) or Ⓦ www.gites-de-france-rhone-alpes.com

Hostels
Auberge de Jeunesse £ On the slopes of Fourvière Hill. Double
rooms from €27–63 (singles €13–31), including breakfast.
ⓐ 41–43 montée de Chemin Neuf ❶ 04 78 15 05 50
Ⓦ www.hihostels.com or www.fuaj.org Ⓝ Metro: Vieux Lyon

THE BEST OF LYON

Most of the areas of Lyon and the attractions you will want to visit in the UNESCO World Heritage area are in walking distance of one another in the Presqu'île, Vieux Lyon and Fourvière districts. But the bus and metro systems are also excellent.

TOP 10 ATTRACTIONS

- **Vieux Lyon (Old Lyon)** The medieval and Renaissance area, a key part of the UNESCO site, is the one that will give you a taste of the city's rich history (see page 60).

- **The food and wine** If you don't like food and wine, you're likely to feel left out in Lyon. At least try a *bouchon* or two, and wash down your food with a *pot* or more of Beaujolais or Côte du Rhône (see page 29).

- **Musée des Beaux-Arts** A fine collection of Impressionists, old masters and antiquities (see page 81).

- **The view from Fourvière Hill** Get the funicular to the top of Fourvière Hill, and enjoy the splendid views of Lyon from the grounds of the basilica (see page 65).

- **Musée des Tissus & Musée des Arts Décoratifs** You will find a rich display of fabrics in the Musée des Tissus, and your ticket also entitles you to visit the neighbouring Musée des Arts Décoratifs (see page 83).

- **Musée de la Civilisation Gallo-Romaine & Théâtre Romain** The theatre (see page 71) is immensely impressive, and the neighbouring museum will give you an idea of the grandeur of Roman civilisation in Lyon (see page 69).

- **The Festival of Lights** The city's main annual event attracts millions of people (see page 14).

- **Basilique St-Martin d'Ainay** This gem of a church is a haven of tranquillity (see page 75).

- **The Painted Walls** Lyon has several amazing painted *trompe-l'oeil* walls featuring local history and characters. One of the best is in rue de la Marinière.

- **The Institut Lumière** Not in the centre of town, but easy to get to by metro. If you love cinema and its history, this is a must (see page 33).

◑ *View over the city of Lyon*

HALF-DAY: LYON IN A HURRY

A visit to Vieux Lyon will easily take up half a day. There's the cathedral and a couple of museums, but wandering around the atmospheric streets and admiring the buildings, maybe discovering a *traboule*, or sitting in a café or two are as attractive an option as visiting the sights.

1 DAY: TIME TO SEE A LITTLE MORE

As well as seeing Vieux Lyon, you should also head up to Fourvière, pop into the basilica, but above all take in the view from its terrace. Then go to the Roman theatre and the Gallo-Roman museum. You should then have time to see a little of the Presqu'île area, perhaps visiting the Beaux-Arts museum.

2–3 DAYS: SHORT CITY BREAK

Spend more time in the Beaux-Arts museum, walk around Presqu'île, possibly visiting place Bellecour and the Musée des Tissus and the Musée des Arts Décoratifs. You might also visit the nearby Basilique St-Martin d'Ainay. You should certainly walk up, or take the metro, to the airy Croix-Rousse district, if you have time, and walk along the River Saône or the Rhône.

LONGER: ENJOYING LYON TO THE FULL

Now you can really relax, enjoy a long lunch or two, and visit the left bank of the Rhône to take in the Halles if you fancy some food shopping, and both the Resistance Museum and Lumière Institute. You could also visit the Cité Internationale, its park, the Contemporary Art museum, and the places mentioned in the Out of Town section (see pages 103–126).

⬤ The Basilique St-Martin d'Ainay dates back to the 11th century

Something for nothing

Lyon isn't an expensive city, but there is plenty you can do that won't cost a penny. Above all, there is plenty of walking: whether wandering around Presqu'île and Vieux Lyon and looking at the architecture, or the banks of the Rhône or Saône. Or you could walk up Fourvière Hill or up to Croix-Rousse. Fourvière also has several green spaces to sit in or roam around. If you visit the terrace of the basilica for the view, you can also sit outside at the Abri du Pèlerin café and picnic there, without having to order anything. And on your way down, you can sit in or stroll round the pretty Jardin de Rosaire, just below the basilica and enjoy the roses.

The grounds of the Roman theatre (but not the Gallo-Roman Museum) are also free to visit or look at (from the roof of the

◆ *Take a stroll along the banks of the Saône*

museum). In Presqu'île, there are several attractive squares to sit in or stroll around, including place des Terreaux, the place Louis Pradel, the place Bellecour and the place Carnot. Croix-Rousse also offers great views of Presqu'île and Vieux Lyon, and – although the grounds aren't open to the public – you can look at the Roman amphitheatre. All of Lyon's many fine churches are also free to visit. And using a hire bike (available at stands around town, with red livery) won't cost you anything if you return it to a stand within 30 minutes. Neither will a look at some of the city's painted walls. Then, of course, there is window-shopping, with a huge range of shops to choose from, or you could mooch around one of Lyon's open-air markets (or the covered Halles) and salivate at the fine food on offer. And, during major festivals, you will often find free street events and performances.

When it rains

It can rain quite a lot in April and October (though usually not more than a day or two at a time), but there is still plenty to do. You can always sit in a café, or have a long lunch, and many places have umbrellas for their outside tables, as well as outdoor heating. And you could spend more time at the Beaux-Arts museum, where you can easily pass a day, with a break in the café. Or go to some of the smaller or further-flung museums such as the Printing Museum (see page 83), the Lumière Institute (see page 33) and the Resistance Museum (see page 20). Since public transport is cheap, frequent and reliable,

CAR PARK CAPERS

In other cities, it might seem bizarre to suggest that you visit the car parks – but not in Lyon. The main ones – all designed by major French architects and artists – have classical music playing, and are like no car parks you have ever seen. The best is République, which opened in 1992 and was designed by architect Pierre Volpus and artist François Morellet. It has random lighting effects. Another interesting one is Terreaux, which was designed by Pierre Favre and features archaeological objects relating to the site on display, as well as six black granite slabs on its floors depicting the history of Lyon by Matt Mulican. The Célestins car park is a collaboration between Michel Targe, Daniel Buren and Jean-Michel Wilmotte. They are all in the Presqu'île area.

you needn't get wet by walking either, particularly if you take the metro. Lyon's excellent range of shops (including the covered arcades of passage de l'Argue and passage Thiaffait) will also provide a refuge. Or you could discover some of the *traboules* (covered passageways through the courtyards of houses) in Vieux Lyon and Croix-Rousse. Theories vary as to quite why these were built (one is that those in Vieux Lyon provided easy access to the River Saône to collect water), but they link streets, and Lyonnais use them as convenient short cuts. *Traboules* are normally marked by a bronze plaque or a lion's head symbol.

🔺 *Take refuge in one of Lyon's pleasant shopping arcades*

On arrival

TIME DIFFERENCES
French clocks follow Central European Time (CET). During Daylight Saving Time (end Mar–end Oct), the clocks are put ahead by 1 hour. In the French summer, at noon, time elsewhere is as follows:

Australia Eastern Standard Time 20.00; Central Standard Time 19.30; Western Standard Time 18.00
New Zealand 22.00
South Africa 12.00
UK and Republic of Ireland 11.00
USA and Canada Newfoundland Time 07.30; Atlantic Canada Time 07.00; Eastern Time 06.00; Central Time 05.00; Mountain Time 04.00; Pacific Time 03.00; Alaska 02.00

ARRIVAL
By air
Lyon's St-Exupéry airport is both modern and swift to get through. It is 25 km (15 miles) outside Lyon, around 30 minutes from the city by taxi (there is a stand outside the departures area), which will cost you €30–50. Otherwise take the Satobus shuttle: every 20 minutes from 05.00–23.40. There is an office in the central hall on level 1. It takes around 30–35 minutes and costs approximately €8. The bus stops at both Part-Dieu and Perrache railway stations, and at the Jean Macé metro station on the east bank of the Rhône. Ⓦ www.lyon.aeroport.fr
Ⓦ www.satobus.com

By rail

There are two mainline stations in Lyon itself: Part-Dieu and Perrache. Part-Dieu, in the suburb of the same name, is on the east bank of the Rhône. It is the station you are most likely to arrive at if you take the Eurostar from London and is well served by public transport. Perrache station, on Presqu'île, is an option if you change trains in Paris rather than Lille. It is much closer to Vieux Lyon, and equally well served by public transport and taxis. There is also a station at St-Exupéry airport, opened in 1994 and designed by Spanish architect Santiago Calatrava, in the shape of a giant bird's wings. ⓦ www.voyages.sncf.com for trains ⓦ www.raileurope.co.uk for bookings from London ⓦ www.multitud.org for details of the local transport system.

By car

You are likely to arrive on the A6, which will take you to the area near Perrache station. If you are driving from the south, the A7 will also take you to the same area. Lyon has several one-way systems, but the city is well signposted. Traffic isn't particularly heavy, except during rush hour. But you really don't need a car in the central part of the city, as it is easier to walk or take public transport. So the best advice is to park your car at one of the public car parks (well signposted) or your hotel during your stay.

CAR HIRE

You will only need to hire a car in Lyon if you want to go out of town. It's often cheaper to organise car hire before you leave. Prices can vary considerably from around €40 to over €100 for a Group A car for a day.

At Perrache station, you will find:

Avis ☎ 08 20 61 16 57 or 08700 100 287 (UK) ⓦ www.avis.fr or www.avis.co.uk

Hertz ☎ 04 78 42 24 85. Also at 102 av Jean Jaurès ☎ 04 72 80 76 76 ⓦ www.hertz.co.uk

National/Citer ☎ 04 78 38 38 42 ⓦ www.citer.fr

Also at the airport:

Budget ☎ 04 72 22 74 74 ⓦ www.budget.com

easyCar ⓦ www.easycar.com

FINDING YOUR FEET

The pace and style of life in Lyon isn't very different from back home. The metro system is easy to navigate, though metro entrances are rather discreetly marked. Crime levels are low, but tourists are always tempting targets for some, particularly in the area around the town hall (Hôtel de Ville). You are also likely to encounter several beggars.

ORIENTATION

Lyon is a pretty easy city to find your way around, once you have noted that Presqu'île is between the Rhône and the Saône, and that Vieux Lyon and Fourvière (up the hill) are across the Saône from Presqu'île. You can easily recognise Vieux Lyon by its cathedral, and Fourvière by its basilica. There are several bridges across both the Rhône and the Saône, and roads running along both sides of the rivers. In Presqu'île, note the main squares such as place des Terreaux and place Bellecour to help you find your way.

IF YOU GET LOST, TRY ...

Do you speak English?
Parlez-vous anglais?
Pahrlayvoo ahnglay?

Is this the way to...?
C'est la bonne direction pour...?
Seh lah bon deerekseeawng poor...?

Can you point to it on my map?
Pouvez-vous me le montrer sur la carte?
Poovehvoo mer ler mawngtreh sewr lah kart?

GETTING AROUND

Lyon is particularly well served by fast, clean and frequent integrated public transport run by TCL (Transport en Commun Lyonnais): whether bus (both trolley and regular), metro (four lines) or the two tram lines running into the eastern suburbs. You can buy tickets at TCL offices, from machines at metro stations, on buses and trams and at many other places such as tobacconists (*tabacs*). On buses and trams insert your ticket into the machines on board, on metro platforms at the barriers. The gates open automatically at the end of your journey. Services run from 05.00–24.00. Ⓦ www.tcl.fr for details and route maps.

Taxis are easy to find at ranks, or by hailing them on the street. Otherwise, your hotel or restaurant will call one for you. Taxis are metered and prices are reasonable.

Taxi Radio Ⓣ 04 72 10 86 86 Ⓦ www.taxilyon.com

Another attractive option in Lyon is cycling. The city has 2,000 hire bikes (with red back wheels) around town. The first 30 minutes are free. You simply pick up the bike at one stand and drop it at another, but have to pay by a special card at a machine in advance, in case you overrun your 30 minutes.

Villefranche

Cuire Ⓒ

Gare de Vaise Ⓓ

Henon

Croix-Rousse

Croix-Paquet

Foch

Valmy

Ⓒ
Hôtel de Ville

Gare de
St-Paul

Cordeliers

Liberté

Gorge de Loup

Fourvière

Vieux Lyon
Cathédrale St-Jean

Guillotière

Bellecour

Saint-André

Minimes

Ampére

Rue de
l'Université

Quai
Claude
Bernard

St-Just

Roanne

Centre
Berhelot

Perrache
Ⓐ Ⓣ1 Ⓣ2

Saône

Rhône

Saône

Rhône

A Communicarta
Style45 design
© Communicarta Ltd 2006 UDN.3
Map user Ref:WZFG/CS/LYS/2006/59/4

Charges are only €0.50 per hour. Check with the tourist office or your hotel for details and pick-up and drop points, or
ⓦ www.velov.grandlyon.com

Lyon has also instituted the use of motorised rickshaws, or Cyclopolitain. They accommodate two people and cost from €1 per person. These are a good way of seeing the city, and run from 11.00–19.00 from Mar–Dec. You get a 10 per cent reduction with a Lyon Card. Cyclopolitain ⓣ 08 26 10 00 03 to book
ⓦ www.cyclopolitain.com

● *A Lyon metro sign*

● *The city at night, including the Cathédrale St-Jean*

Vieux Lyon (Old Lyon) & Fourvière Hill

Lyon's UNESCO World Heritage Site – listed in 1998 – covers an area of 500 hectares (1,235 acres). In central Lyon, it includes Vieux Lyon, Fourvière Hill and part of Presqu'île. Of all these areas, the one you are most likely to visit first is Vieux Lyon for its architecture and cobbled streets: one of the finest sites of its type, with over 300 houses dating from the Renaissance period.

Fourvière Hill is most easily reached by the funicular from the Vieux Lyon metro stop at the end of the av Adolphe Max. It was once the centre of the Roman city of Lugdunum, but later housed many Catholic religious institutions (locals called it 'the praying hill' as opposed to Croix-Rousse, which was 'the working hill'). Many of these eventually became schools, which is why you will see so many children in the district.

SIGHTS & ATTRACTIONS

Vieux Lyon is technically divided into three areas: St-Paul to the north, St-Jean in the middle, and St-Georges to the south. Streets are interrupted by a number of pleasant and lively squares that run between them. If you only have a short time, stick to the St-Jean and St-Paul quarters. There are a couple of museums, the Musée Gadagne and the Musée International de la Miniature, and the cathédrale, St-Jean, all of which you might want to visit. But above all you will want to walk (there's no other option) around the streets with their tall, often pastel-coloured, buildings and sit in one of the many restaurants and cafés to watch the world go by. Because of the fact that many wealthy Italian merchants moved into the area during the Renaissance, several of the buildings are reminiscent of those found in Italy at the time.

When you walk around, note some of the fine doors, and enter the buildings with bronze plaques outside (the text telling you their history is in English as well as French) to see their courtyards, galleries and impressive spiral stairways. Most of these buildings now contain social housing, but the deal is that visitors are allowed to look at their public areas. You can also discover the quarter's *traboules* (passageways, often with vaulted ceilings running through houses to link streets) marked in the same way. Some of them are private, but canny locals know the entry codes. It's worth getting a list of *traboules* open to the public from the tourist office. You can also go on a guided tour of *traboules*, organised by the tourist office.

SAVED FROM DESTRUCTION

It's astonishing to think that the area, now so full of visitors, once came close to being pulled down to make way for low cost housing! By the mid-20th century, Vieux Lyon was completely run down, and plans to demolish it emerged after World War II. But local groups protested, and it was ultimately saved by the intervention of French culture minister André Malraux in 1964. After that, the area underwent an extensive programme of restoration and revitalisation through tax incentives. In fact, parts of the old town are still being renovated.

Metro Stop
Cathedral
Information
Police Station
Airport
Railway Stn
Hospital

Jardin des Chartreux

QUAI
VINCENT
SAINT
La Saône
QUAI
PIERRE
SCIZE
PLACE
BOURGNEUF
RUE DU DOCTEUR RAFIN
RUE
DE
MONTAUBAN
FOURVIÈRE
Fourvière
Aventures
Parc des
Hauteurs
MONTÉE
Cimetière
de Loyasse
Fourvière
PLACE DU
158EME RÉGIMENT
D'INFANTERIE
Basilique
Notre-Dame
de Fourvière
PLACE DE
FOURVIÈRE
RUE PAULINE
Musée de Fourvière
Le
Verger
RUE HENRI LE CHATELIER
MARIE JARROT
LA SARRA
RUE CLÉBERG
ROGER
RADISSON
RUE
Musée de la
Civilisation
Gallo-Romaine
RUE DE TRION QUAILLE
MONTÉE
RUE
Théâtre
Romain
Minimes
DU
TELEGRAPHE
MONTÉE DU
CHEMIN NEUF
Funicular
PLACE
DES
MINIMES
MONTÉE DU
GOURGUILLON
**Vieux Lyon and
Fourvière Hill**
0   200 metres
0   200 yards
St-Just
ST-GEORGES

● *Explore Lyon's intriguing* traboules

Fourvière Hill is a generally quiet area, but contains two major sights: the basilica, one of Lyon's main landmarks, and the Roman theatre with the adjoining Gallo-Roman museum. There is also the small Musée de Fourvière, with religious exhibits – which you might choose to skip, particularly if you are pressed for time. The funicular stop is opposite the entrance to the basilica.

Basilique Notre-Dame de Fourvière (Fourvière Basilica)
This massive white wedding cake was completed on the site of the old Roman forum in 1896. Designed by Pierre Bossan, it was built next to a chapel that was originally constructed in the 12th century, dedicated to the Virgin Mary – patron saint of Lyon – as a result of a public subscription that was started after the Franco-Prussian War of 1870–71. It is nicknamed 'the upside down elephant' by locals. You will either love it or find the lavish decoration of the interior, including the many mosaics, somewhat overdone. You can get an even better view than the one from the crowded terrace, by going to the top of the basilica's observatory tower (small charge). The Jardin de Rosaire (Rosary Garden), just below, leads down to Vieux Lyon – the route is marked by small rose-shaped plaques in the path.
ⓐ pl de Fourvière ⓛ basilica 08.00–19.00; observatory 10.30–12.00, 14.00–18.30 Wed–Sun, Apr–Sept; 13.30–17.30 Sat & Sun, Oct–Mar ⓜ Funicular: Fourvière

Cathédrale St-Jean
Built between the 12th and 15th centuries, the cathedral dominates Vieux Lyon, and can also be seen from the Saône.

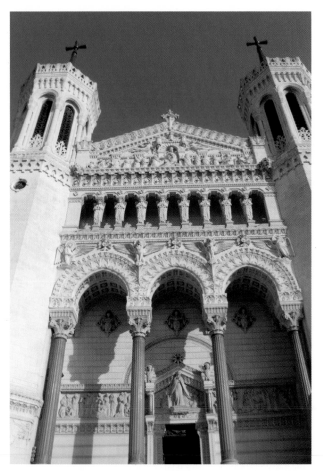

🔺 The lavish Basilique Notre-Dame de Fourvière

It gained great importance as the bishop's seat. The architecture is a mixture of Romanesque (the apse and choir) and Gothic. Note the stained-glass windows (some of them in complex geometrical patterns), particularly the exquisite rose windows. Also seek out the most unusual 16th-century astronomical clock in the north transept, which chimes at 12.00, 14.00, 15.00 and 16.00. The Romanesque early 12th-century *Manécanterie* (choir school), on the right of the nave, houses a treasury of valuable objects both religious and secular. You will see that many of the statues decorating the west front of the cathedral have no heads – they were knocked off by Protestants during the Wars of Religion.

ⓐ pl St-Jean ☏ 04 78 92 82 29 ⓦ www.cathedrale-lyon.cef.fr
🕐 08.00–12.00, 14.00–19.00 Ⓝ Metro: Vieux Lyon

Fourvière Aventures

The only adventure park in Lyon, not far from the basilica, with activities for children aged four and upwards, as well as some that adults can share.

ⓐ Piste de la Sarra, 3 pl du 158ème Rgt d'Infanterie ☏ 08 20 10 00 10 ⓦ www.fourviere-aventures.com 🕐 for last entrance 13.00–17.00 Sat & Sun, Apr–June; 10.00–18.00 Mon–Sun, July–Aug; 10.00–17.00 Sat & Sun, Sept; 13.00–16.00 Sat & Sun, Oct–mid-Nov, closed mid-Nov–Mar Ⓝ Funicular: Fourvière. Admission charge

Main squares

The main squares all have lively cafés. In the place du Change is the former 16th-century financial exchange, modified in the

18th century. It became a Protestant church in 1803. Also look out for the Maison Thomassin (no.2), originally built in the 15th century by a wealthy cloth merchant. The place du Gouvernement once housed the local governor. The place St-Paul has a small church, Église St-Paul, dating from early medieval times, but much restored over the centuries. The interior has both Romanesque and Gothic elements.

Main streets

The key streets to visit are the main street, rue St-Jean, the rue du Boeuf (named because there is a statue of a bull, above eye level, in the street), rue Juiverie and the rue Lainerie (where cloth merchants lived, and where there is a renovated 15th-century house at no. 10). You will find the longest *traboule* in Vieux Lyon running from 54 rue St-Jean to 27 rue du Boeuf. There is an impressive gallery, designed by 16th-century local architect Philibert Delorme, in the courtyard of no. 8 rue Juiverie. Admire the Renaissance courtyard at no. 4. This street, which has several other buildings to look at, gets its name from the fact that it was once home to the city's Jewish population, who were expelled in the 14th century. The mansions of Italian bankers later lined this street.

CULTURE

Guignol de Lyon

The young Zonzons theatre company presents productions (around an hour long) featuring Lyon's famous puppet character, Guignol, created in the early 19th century, and the French equivalent of

Punch. The theatre also houses a collection of puppets.

🄰 2 rue Louis Carrand 🄒 04 78 28 92 57 🄦 www.guignol-lyon.com 🄓 performances Wed, Sat & Sun 🄝 Metro: Vieux Lyon. Admission charge (reductions for children)

Musée da la Civilisation Gallo-Romaine (Gallo-Roman Museum)

Next to the Roman theatre (see page 71), this concrete museum, built into the side of a hill in the 1970s – designed by architect Bernard Zehrfuss – has a bunker-like appearance from the outside, and looks distinctly unpromising. But step inside, and you will find well-lit displays of Roman architecture and artefacts from Lugdunum and other sites in a most unusual space that slopes down five levels from the entrance floor. There are some fine mosaics, and views of the Roman theatre from large windows. You can also get a very good view of the theatre from the roof of the museum.

🄰 7 rue Cléberg 🄒 04 72 38 49 30 🄓 10.00–18.00 Tues–Sun, Mar–Oct; 10.00–17.00 Tues–Sun, Nov–Feb 🄝 Funicular: Fourvière. Admission charge

Musée Gadagne

Built by the wealthy Florentine Gadagne banking family in the early 16th century, this is perhaps the most important Renaissance house in Vieux Lyon. It now houses the museum of Lyon's history and a puppet museum. It is closed for extensive renovation at the time of writing, but should reopen in late 2007, with 38 rooms of exhibits, a café and a shop.

🄰 1 pl du Petit Collège 🄒 04 72 56 74 06 🄦 www.museegadagne. com 🄓 10.45–18.00 Wed–Mon 🄝 Metro: Vieux Lyon

Musée International de la Miniature
(International Miniatures Museum)

Housed in one of Vieux Lyon's most imposing buildings, a former 16th-century inn, later restored by a group of local lawyers (hence its name), this museum – featuring a large and impressive collection of miniature models of buildings and interiors – opened in 2005. Apart from the chance to look inside the building, the beautifully detailed models might well fascinate both you and older children.

ⓐ Maison des Avocats, 60 rue St-Jean ① 04 72 00 24 77
ⓦ www.mimlyon.com ① 10.00–19.00 (last admission 18.00)
Ⓝ Metro: Vieux Lyon. Admission charge

● Concerts are held at the ancient Théâtre Romain de Fourvière

Théâtre Romain (Roman Theatre)

The Roman theatre, next to the Gallo-Roman Museum, is one of the finest and oldest of ancient Gaul, originally dating from 15 BC, and later expanded by Emperor Hadrian in the 2nd century. It could hold 10,000 people at one time, and is now used for concerts, particularly during the Nuits de Fourvière festival (see page 12) in June and July. It is 108 m (354 ft) in diameter and is situated next to the Odéon, a much smaller auditorium (once seating 3,000), where the Romans listened to music. You can walk around both.

ⓐ 7 rue Cléberg ⓛ 09.00–dusk ⓝ Funicular: Fourvière

RETAIL THERAPY

There are very few opportunities for shopping in Fourvière, and the shops in Vieux Lyon are mostly functional or touristy. There are, however, some good craft shops to discover as you stroll around, including:

Art-Peaux Creation Selling colourful leather goods, including shoes, handbags and belts. ⓐ 21 rue des Trois Maries ⓣ 04 78 37 64 89

Les Routes de la Soie A silk workshop selling hand-printed items. ⓐ 19 rue St-Jean ⓣ 04 72 56 08 21

Soierie Saint Georges Hand-painted and printed silk, and traditionally-made velvet. ⓐ 11 rue Mourguet ⓣ 04 72 40 25 13

TAKING A BREAK

Banana's £ ❶ Get a crêpe, a salad or ice cream, and a drink, in this lively place. ⓐ 1 pl du Gouvernement ❶ 04 72 40 94 98 ⓛ until 01.00 Sat and in summer, closed Mon
Ⓝ Metro: Vieux Lyon

Café Comptoir £ ❷ Run by the redoubtable Mimi, this is an animated bar full of locals and students. Cosy and crowded, with old advertising signs on the tobacco-stained walls. Wooden tables, with jazz playing in the background. Salads and omelettes, and a *plat du jour* in the evening. ⓐ 68 rue St-Jean ❶ 04 78 38 09 34 ⓛ closed Mon & Tues Ⓝ Metro: Vieux Lyon

Nardone £ ❸ Under a painted wall, by the Saône, generally regarded as the best ice cream parlour in Lyon. ⓐ 3 pl Ennemond-Fousseret ❶ 04 78 28 29 09 Ⓝ Metro: Vieux Lyon

Petit Rabelais £ ❹ Right in front of the cathedral, serving local dishes and drinks at surprisingly reasonable prices for the location. They also have a children's menu. ⓐ 8 bis pl St-Jean ❶ 04 78 38 18 79 ⓛ closed Mon Ⓝ Metro: Vieux Lyon

Le Restaurant de Fourvière £–££ ❺ You can get a full meal (local cuisine) or something lighter, and enjoy the fabulous view from the terrace. Or just go for a drink outside of dining hours. Next to the basilica: it can get full if there are tourist groups around. ⓐ 9 pl de Fourvière ❶ 04 78 25 21 15 Ⓝ Funicular: Fourvière

Les Retrouvailles ££ ❻ A friendly place with excellent, tasty cooking. ❸ 38 rue du Boeuf ❶ 04 78 42 68 84 ● closed lunchtimes & Sun evening Ⓝ Metro: Vieux Lyon

La Tour Rose ££ ❼ Have some tapas or antipasto or a drink in the stylish lounge downstairs or a more formal meal in the swish, bright brasserie upstairs. ❸ 22 rue du Boeuf ❶ 04 78 92 69 10 Ⓝ Metro: Vieux Lyon

AFTER DARK

Restaurants
Le Baduila £–££ ❽ Good pizza and French dishes based on what's available from the market. Lively restaurant and bar. ❸ 6 pl St-Paul ❶ 04 78 28 16 90 ● normally open till 01.00 (but food service ends around 22.00 during the week, later at weekends), closed Mon evening & Sun Ⓝ Metro: Vieux Lyon

Notre Maison £–££ ❾ Run by a husband and wife team, a warm *bouchon* serving hearty local specialities. You're expected to take your time over your meal as the locals do. ❸ 2 rue de Gadagne ❶ 04 72 41 78 48 ● closed Sun & lunchtimes Ⓝ Metro: Vieux Lyon

Les Adrets ££ ❿ A favourite of inhabitants of Vieux Lyon, with rustic décor and a great deal of charm. The temptingly presented food makes a change from some of the local tourist traps. ❸ 30 rue du Boeuf ❶ 04 78 38 24 30 ● closed Sat & Sun

La Mâchonnerie ££ ⓫ High quality, traditional Lyonnais food.
ⓐ 36 rue Tramassac ⓣ 04 78 42 24 62 ⓛ closed Sun & weekday
lunch ⓜ Metro: Vieux Lyon

Christian Têtedoie ££–£££ ⓬ One of the most celebrated of the
younger generation of Lyon chefs produces his inventive cuisine
in this smart place by the Saône. ⓐ 54 quai Pierre Scize
ⓣ 04 78 29 40 10 ⓛ closed Mon, Sat lunch, Sun & Aug
ⓜ Metro: Hôtel de Ville

Les Terraces de Lyon £££ ⓭ You can eat the refined and
flavourful cuisine of exceptionally talented chef Davy Tissot
here. Choose to do this at the Villa Florentine hotel (see page 41)
either in the luxurious restaurant or, weather permitting,
on the terrace, with its great views over Lyon. ⓐ 25 montée
St-Barthélemy ⓣ 04 72 56 56 56 ⓜ Metro: Vieux Lyon

Bars & clubs

There are few evening activities in Vieux Lyon, and even fewer
in Fourvière, and very little late night action, apart from on
Saturdays (but even then bars tend to close by 01.00).
However, try:

Café Mode A lively student haunt. ⓐ 8 rue Mgr Lavarenne
ⓣ 04 78 37 96 06 ⓛ 17.00–03.00, until 01.00 Sun & Mon
ⓜ Metro: Vieux Lyon

Presqu'île

Presqu'île (the name means 'almost island') is the peninsula between the Rhône and the Saône, and is the heart of modern Lyon. It is also a bustling administrative and commercial centre, with shops, banks, offices and restaurants at every turn. Many of Lyon's key sights and attractions are located here.

It starts to the north with the place des Terreaux, from which the mostly pedestrianised rue de la République runs to the place Bellecour, passing by the place des Cordeliers, the place des Jacobins and the place de la République. Beyond the place Bellecour is another pedestrianised road, the rue Victor Hugo, running to the place Carnot and Perrache railway station. The area between place des Terreaux and place Carnot is part of the UNESCO World Heritage Site. To cover this stretch by foot takes around 30–40 minutes. If you want to avoid the centre, you can always walk along the banks of the Rhône or Saône. Beyond Perrache station the Lyon Confluence Project, in an area formerly occupied by factories and railway yards, is being developed with planned new leisure and cultural venues, hotels, museums (including a life sciences museum due to open during 2007), shops and houses. The project is due to be completed in 2015.

SIGHTS & ATTRACTIONS

Basilique St-Martin d'Ainay

This Romanesque former Benedictine abbey was built during the 11th and 12th centuries, and once wielded great power, but it became a parish church in 1780. A palace built in the grounds of

Presqu'île

| 0 | 150 metres |
| 0 | 150 yards |

Jardin des Chartreux

RUE DE LA VIEILLE

QUAI SAINT VINCENT

PONT DE LA FEUILLÉE

La Saône

QUAI PIERRE SCIZE

PLACE BOURGNEUF

RUE DE MONTAUBAN

RUE SAINT PAUL

PLACE SAINT-PAUL

QUAI DE BONDY

ST-PAUL

FOURVIÈRE

Parc des Hauteurs

RUE BARTHÉLÉMY

RUE DE LA LOGE

PLACE DU CHANGE

PLACE DU GOUVERNEMENT

Fourvière

Basilique Notre-Dame de Fourvière

MONTÉE SAINT BARTHÉLÉMY

MONTÉE DES CHAZEAUX

RUE DU BŒUF

RUE SAINT JEAN

QUAI ROMAIN ROLLAND

PLACE DE FOURVIÈRE

Musée de Fourvière

Jardin du Rosaire

ST-JEAN

RUE DE LA BOMBARDE

LA SARRA

Le Verger

PLACE SAINT-JEAN

Cathédrale Saint-Jean

RUE ROGER RADISSON

RUE CLEBERG

Musée de la Civilisation Gallo-Romaine

Vieux Lyon

AVE ADOLPHE MAX

PONT BONAPARTE

RUE DE L'ANTIQUAILLE

Minimes

MONTÉE DU CHEMIN NEUF

RUE SAINT-GEORGES

RUE DU DOYENNÉ

QUAI FULCHIRON

TILSITT

Théâtre Romain

MONTÉE DU GOURGUILLON

PLACE F. BERTRAS

MONTÉE DU TÉLÉGRAPHE

Funicular

PLACE DES MINIMES

QUAI

PASSERELLE ABBÉ COUTURIER

RUE

SALA

St-Just

RUE DES FARGES

ST-GEORGES

La Saône

VAUBECOUR RUE SAINTE HÉLÈNE

PLACE ABBÉ LARUE

RUE VICTOR HUGO

M	Metro Stop
✝	Cathedral
i	Information
◐	Police Station
✈	Airport
🚉	Railway Stn
✚	Hospital

Basilique St-Martin d'Ainay

Ampère Victor Hugo M

76

the monastery in the 14th century was destroyed in the Revolution, and the church turned into a warehouse. It reopened in 1802, and was subsequently restored later in the 19th century. The central part of the church, however, dates from the 12th century, with the chapel of St-Blandine (to the right of the apse) dating from around the 11th century. The church is one of the most attractive in the whole of Lyon, mainly for its essential simplicity. Note the decorations on the ceiling, and the striking murals.

ⓐ pl d'Ainay ☏ 04 72 40 02 50 ⏱ 08.30–12.00, 14.30–18.00
Ⓜ Metro: Ampère Victor Hugo

Place Bellecour

The huge place Bellecour with its red gravel is Lyon's biggest square, measuring 310 m by 200 m (1,017 ft by 656 ft). It was

---

PLACE DES TERREAUX

The 17th-century pl des Terreaux houses both the Musée des Beaux-Arts (see page 81) and the impressive Hôtel de Ville (town hall). Apart from its buildings and cafés with outdoor tables, the main feature of the square is a large fountain, installed in 1894. Featuring a chariot and four horses, it was originally designed some years earlier for Bordeaux by Bartholdi, the sculptor of the Statue of Liberty. However, it wasn't wanted by the people of Bordeaux, and so was sold to Lyon. The steam coming out of the horses' nostrils is a recent innovation. The square also has tiny modern fountains gushing up from the pavements throughout its length.

once a military parade ground. In the square itself, on the southeast side, is the tourist office. The square is the scene of many events and activities during the year, and there are often marquees erected there. The equestrian statue you will see is of Louis XIV, dating from 1828 – an earlier statue of the king on the site was destroyed during the French Revolution. It is a popular meeting place, where locals converge 'under the tail of the horse'. Immediately to the east of place Bellecour is the vast main post office. If you go south from place Bellecour, you will reach the Musée des Tissus and the Musée des Arts Décoratifs (see page 83). Nearby is the beautiful basilica of St-Martin d'Ainay (see page 75). The handsome residential area around it is much quieter and more low key than the streets north of place Bellecour.

Église St-Nizier (Church of St-Nizier)
In the heart of Presqu'île, and built in the 14th and 15th centuries on the site of an earlier church commemorating the Christian martyrs of Lyon, this is perhaps the finest and best known church in Lyon, and an oustanding example of French flamboyant Gothic architecture. The Renaissance doorway is 16th century, and the south tower 19th century. It looks particularly impressive when floodlit at night.
ⓐ pl St-Nizier (rue Chenavard) ⓣ 04 72 41 18 05 ⓛ 10.00–12.00, 14.30–18.30, closed Mon morning ⓜ Metro: Hôtel de Ville

Opera House
Behind the town hall is Lyon's famous opera house. Only the classical façade, statues of eight Muses, and part of the bar on

the first floor remain from the original 19th-century building. The rest was gutted and modernised by architect Jean Nouvel, who also added a giant curved black glass roof. The area below the roof contains dance studios and a restaurant. The interior of the building, including the auditorium, is almost entirely black. It reopened in 1993. Part of it is lit in red at night. The squares to the north side of it contain a modern fountain and sculptures.

ⓐ 1 pl de la Comédie ⓣ 04 72 00 45 45 ⓦ www.opera-lyon.org
ⓝ Metro: Hôtel de Ville

🔺 *The Opera House is a fascinating mix of classical and modern*

Rue de la République

The rue de la République is full of shops, mainly chain stores. To the west of rue de la République, just before the place des Cordeliers, are the Musée de l'Imprimerie (see page 83), and the church of St-Nizier (see page 79). To the east is the huge 19th-century neoclassical Palais du Commerce (chamber of commerce). On the place des Cordeliers is the 15th-century church of St-Bonaventure. A little further south, to the west of the rue de la République, is the pedestrianised rue Mercière, once one of the most important mercantile streets in Lyon, now full of restaurants. A small passageway, leading to the Saône, comes off it. Further along is the place des Célestins, which once housed a monastery, but is now home of Lyon's celebrated belle époque Théâtre des Célestins. To the east, on the banks of the Rhône, is the Hôtel Dieu hospital. The building, with its 375-m (1,230-ft) façade and huge dome, mostly dates from the 18th century, though there was a hospital on the site several centuries earlier. The hospital also houses a museum (see page 82).

CULTURE

Musée des Beaux-Arts (Fine Arts Museum)

This is one of the finest art galleries in France, renovated in 1998, with a collection spread over 70 rooms in a 17th-century former Benedictine convent. You realise you are in for something special the minute you enter the courtyard garden (a favourite picnic spot for students) and the cloisters, with sculptures by Rodin, among others. The museum's ground floor also has some fine 19th- and 20th-century sculptures. Reached by a grand staircase, the first floor houses the beautifully displayed and high quality collection of antiquities – all in strikingly good condition – as well as decorative arts objects. There is also a bookshop and a modern café with a terrace, adorned by Raoul Dufy's huge *Le Seine, de Paris à la Mer*. The second floor houses the museum's comprehensive collection of paintings – from the 15th to the 20th centuries – with works by masters from around Europe such as Veronese, Rubens and Rembrandt, as well as leading French artists including David and Delacroix. Lyonnais painters are also represented. For many, the highlight is the collection of Impressionists, the second best in France. Look out also for the Delubac bequest – made in the 1980s – of 35 works by leading 20th-century painters including Picasso, Braque and Francis Bacon. The museum also has temporary exhibitions. If you only have a short time, confine yourself to either the antiquities or the Impressionist and 20th-century sections.

ⓐ 20 pl des Terreaux ① 04 72 10 17 40 ⓦ www.mairie-lyon.fr ⓛ 10.00–18.00 Sat–Thur, 10.30–18.00 Fri, closed Tues and public holidays, last entry 30 minutes before closing, some sections also closed at lunchtime Ⓜ Metro: Hôtel de Ville. Admission charge

Musée des Hospices Civils de Lyon (Hospital Museum)

In the Hôtel Dieu hospital, this is a museum of the history of medicine and hospital life in Lyon from the Renaissance to the present day.

ⓐ 1 pl de l' Hôpital ① 04 72 41 30 42 ⓛ 10.00–12.00, 13.00–17.30 Tues–Fri, July–Sept, closed Mon morning; 13.30–17.30 first and third Sun of month, Oct–June (entrance 61 quai Courmont) Ⓜ Metro: Bellecour

Musée d'Imprimerie (Printing Museum)

Housed in the magnificent 15th-century Hôtel de la Couronne, which was once Lyon's town hall. Not a must-see, but fascinating if you are interested in the history of books and printing, with some rare exhibits. It's a testimony to Lyon's importance as the city where France's first printed book was produced in 1476.

ⓐ 13 rue de la Poulaillerie ⓣ 04 78 37 65 98 ⓦ www.bm-lyon.fr
ⓛ 09.30–12.00, 14.00–18.00, closed Mon, Tues & public holidays
ⓜ Metro: Cordeliers. Admission charge

Musée des Tissus & Musée des Arts Décoratifs (Textile Museum & Museum of Decorative Arts)

The Textile Museum is one of the highlights of Lyon, showcasing textiles in a collection spanning 2,000 years, including ancient fabrics (look particularly for the stunning Coptic cloth featuring a fish design). The collection has well-displayed exhibits from around the world, as well as covering silk-making in Lyon. There are also temporary exhibitions, including the work of major designers. The grand 18th-century building itself was the residence of Lyon's governor until the Revolution.

Housed in the Hôtel Lacroix-Laval, a mansion built in 1739, the Museum of Decorative Arts contains a collection of mainly 18th-century French furniture that is very much at home in the building, some rooms of which are fully furnished. It also houses gold- and silverware, Italian majolica from the 15th and 16th centuries, Renaissance tapestries, faience, clocks and musical instruments, including a lovely harpsichord.

Entry to both museums (joint ticket) is via the Textile Museum.

ⓐ 34 rue de la Charité ⓣ 04 78 38 42 00 ⓦ www.musee-des-tissus.com ⓛ 10.00–17.30 (Textile) 10.00–12.00, 14.00–17.30 (Decorative Arts), both Tues–Sun, closed public holidays. Ⓜ Metro: Ampère Victor Hugo. Admission charge

🔺 The Musée des Tissus displays an impressive collection of textiles

RETAIL THERAPY

André Claude Canova Making and selling items made of silk, cotton and wool – which can be personalised or made to order. ⓐ 26 quai St-Vincent ⓣ 04 78 30 43 42

L'Atelier de Soierie A silk printing workshop downstairs (you can watch demonstrations) with a shop upstairs selling colourful scarves, ties, handkerchiefs and shawls with imaginative designs. ⓐ 33 rue Romarin ⓣ 04 72 07 97 83 ⓛ 09.00–12.00, 14.00–19.00 Mon–Sat

Bourgeot Traiteur One of the best delicatessens in Lyon. ⓐ 20 rue de la Charité ⓣ 04 72 77 79 09

Daum High quality crystal and glassware. ⓐ 12 bis rue des Archers ⓣ 04 78 37 11 95

FNAC A branch of the famous French book and music chain. Tickets for some events are also available. ⓐ 85 rue de la République ⓣ 04 72 40 49 49 ⓛ 10.00–19.30 Mon–Sat

Framboise Imaginative costume jewellery. Also accessories and candles. ⓐ 47 rue Franklin ⓣ 04 78 38 39 57

Marilyn Overflowing with old dolls, puppets, china, silverware and a host of other eclectic items. ⓐ 55 rue Auguste Comte ⓣ 04 72 41 88 12 ⓛ 15.00–20.00 Mon–Sat

Palomas A chocolatier and confectioner since 1917. 2 rue Colonel Chambonnet 04 78 37 74 60

Le Printemps One of France's leading department stores, specialising in fashion, accessories, beauty products and items for the home. 42 rue de la République 04 72 41 29 29 09.30–19.00 Mon–Sat

Sophie Guyot Clothing, jewellery and accessories by this prize-winning local designer. rue Saint Polycarpe 04 72 07 79 60

TAKING A BREAK

Café Leff £ ❶ Sit outside and enjoy a plate of mussels and chips, or a salad. 1 pl des Terreaux 04 78 27 27 07 Metro: Hôtel de Ville

🔺 *Treat yourself to fine Lyonnais silk from the Atelier de Soierie*

L'Harmonie des Vins £ ❷ As the name suggests, wine is the thing here, with snacks and more to accompany it. ⓐ 9 rue Neuve ⓣ 04 72 98 85 59 ⓛ 10.00–01.00 Tues–Sat ⓝ Metro: Cordeliers

Les Arcades £–££ ❸ Just to one side of the opera house, this bar and brasserie (and its terrace) attracts custom all day long. Try one of the huge salads, a traditional dish or some of their oriental offerings. ⓐ 15 pl Louis Pradel ⓣ 04 78 30 19 80 ⓛ 11.00– 24.00 (last orders for food 22.00) ⓝ Metro: Hôtel de Ville

Le Petit Léon £–££ ❹ Attached to the grand and gastronomic Léon de Lyon, this attractive place serves bistro food of the highest quality. ⓐ 3 rue Pléney ⓣ 04 72 10 11 11 ⓛ lunch only, Tues–Sat ⓝ Metro: Hôtel de Ville

Winch £–££ ❺ A wood panelled interior with a nautical theme plus outdoor seating. You can get a salad, an omelette or something more substantial. You can also get a drink after lunch or dinner. ⓐ 62 rue Mercière ⓣ 04 78 37 23 65 ⓛ closed Sun dinner ⓝ Metro: Cordeliers

Les Muses de l'Opéra ££ ❻ In the glass roof of the opera house, with splendid views of Lyon. Serving a mixture of modern, traditional and international dishes. ⓐ 1 pl de la Comédie ⓣ 04 72 00 45 58 ⓛ 12.00–14.00, 20.00–22.00 Mon–Sat ⓝ Metro: Hôtel de Ville

AFTER DARK

Restaurants

Le Bistrot de Lyon ££ ❼ A busy, traditional brasserie (with tables outside) dating from 1896, with belle époque décor. Good fish and seafood, as well as meat. ⓐ 64 rue Mercière ⓣ 04 78 38 47 47 Ⓝ Metro: Cordeliers

Café des Fédérations ££ ❽ One of Lyon's best-known *bouchons*, with a jolly atmosphere and local cuisine. ⓐ 10 rue Major-Martin ⓣ 04 78 28 26 00 Ⓛ Mon–Fri Ⓝ Metro: Hôtel de Ville

Chabert et Fils ££ ❾ A large *bouchon* known for its duck liver 'gâteau'. ⓐ 11 rue des Marronniers ⓣ 04 78 37 01 94 Ⓛ late service until 23.00 Ⓝ Metro: Bellecour

Chez Georges ££ ❿ Run by a friendly husband and wife team, and one of the best *bouchons* in Lyon (it's small and always packed), serving generous portions of typical Lyonnais food – that you are expected to finish. ⓐ 8 rue Garet ⓣ 04 78 28 30 46 Ⓛ Mon–Fri Ⓝ Metro: Hôtel de Ville

Gaston ££ ⓫ Designed around a farmhouse theme (also tables outside), go for the big portions of excellent grills and roasts, served with Dauphinoise potatoes or chips. Friendly service. ⓐ 41 rue Mercière ⓣ 04 72 41 87 86 Ⓛ 12.00–23.30 Ⓝ Metro: Cordeliers

Mercière ££ ⓬ Choose from traditional dishes such as *coq au vin*, Lyonnais specialities or more eclectic dishes. The set menus

are very good value. ⓐ 56 rue Mercière ⓣ 04 78 37 67 35
ⓛ 12.00–14.15, 19.00–23.00 ⓝ Metro: Cordeliers

Nicolas le Bec £££ ⓭   One of Lyon's most celebrated younger
chefs serves modern, most unusual and inventive dishes (such
as apple poached in brine, and foie gras grilled with hibiscus
juice) in a formal setting. ⓐ 14 rue Grôlée ⓣ 04 78 42 15 00
ⓛ Tues–Sat (last orders 21.30), closed early Jan, three weeks Aug
ⓝ Metro: Cordeliers

Bars
L'Ambassade A small but very lively nightclub. ⓐ 4 rue Stella
ⓣ 04 78 42 23 23 ⓛ 23.00–05.00 Wed–Sat
ⓝ Metro: Cordeliers

Le Comptoir de la Bourse A smart and extremely popular
cocktail bar. ⓐ 33 rue de la Bourse ⓣ 04 72 41 71 52 ⓛ until 03.00
Mon–Sat ⓝ Metro: Cordeliers

Elle Chic and full of young professionals. ⓐ 2 rue de la Monnaie
ⓣ 04 78 42 92 83 ⓝ Metro: Bellecour

Le Habana Café Rum, cocktails and Latin music in this vibrant
club. ⓐ 53 rue Mercière ⓣ 04 78 42 54 52 ⓛ 22.30–03.00
ⓝ Metro: Cordeliers

Palais de la Bière A wood panelled beer bar, with a wide
selection to choose from. ⓐ 1 rue Terme ⓣ 04 78 27 94 00
ⓛ 18.00–02.00 Tues–Sat ⓝ Metro: Hôtel de Ville

Le Voxx A hip bar by the Saône, with a terrace. **a** 1 rue Algérie **t** 04 78 28 33 87 **c** until 03.00 **m** Metro: Hôtel de Ville

Other evening entertainment
Opéra National de Lyon The opera house mounts impressive major productions of international quality. You may need to book ahead. **a** 1 pl de la Comédie **t** 04 72 00 45 45 **w** www.opera-lyon.org **m** Metro: Hôtel de Ville

Théâtre des Célestins Lyon's main theatre, in a magnificent building, with a classical repertoire. **a** 4 rue Charles Dullin **t** 04 72 77 40 00 **w** www.celestins-lyon.org **m** Metro: Bellecour

▲ *The atmospheric Bistrot de Lyon*

Croix-Rousse

The essentially residential Croix-Rousse quarter has a village-like atmosphere, and is much loved by its inhabitants, who see themselves as Croix-Roussien first and Lyonnais second. It is a mixed area, with residents in different income brackets, including Algerian immigrants. As one of Lyon's most pleasant areas, it is being gentrified – though some of it is still run-down – and has become a favourite with 'Bo-Bos' (*bourgeois-bohèmes*), well-off arty types. The name of the area, meaning 'russet cross', refers to a stone cross that stood here before the Revolution.

The slopes of Croix-Rousse, but not the plateau above, are part of the UNESCO World Heritage Site, but there are very few formal sites to visit. Instead, go for the relaxed atmosphere, and the views of the rest of Lyon. You probably won't spend more than half a day here. You can reach Croix-Rousse from Presqu'île by walking uphill (there are several sets of steps that will take you to the top of the hill) or take the metro (to Croix-Rousse).

Head directly south from Croix-Rousse metro station to the end of the rue des Pierres Plantées for outstanding views of Vieux Lyon and Fourvière. Next to the viewing point is a small park, and steps leading down the hill. There are also several other viewing points in Croix-Rousse.

If you decide to walk up (or down) the hill, try to visit the charming place Sathonay, with its *boules* pitch, fountains and fashionable cafés – one of the most pleasant squares in Lyon.

Croix-Rousse

0 |————————————| 150 metres
0 |————————————| 150 yards

RUE HÉNON
PLACE C
FLAMMARION
RUE HÉNON

LA CROIX-ROUSSE

RUE HÉNON
RUE DANCON
RUE HENRI FERRÉ
PLACE E. CHANEL
RUE BOUCHON
RUE PHILIPPE

RUE JEAN REVEL

Parc Francis Popy

RUE HENRI
RUE BARODET

RUE BOURNES

RUE JACQUARD
RUE DE
RUE ROUSSY
RUE CORLUS
RUE DEVIENNE

Jardin Public La Cerisaie

RUE COIGNET

RUE LASSALLE
RUE CLAUDE
BONNET
RUE GRATALOUP
PLACE TABAREAU

PLACE E. MILLAUD

SERIN

RUE BLETON

CROIX-ROUSSE

Parc Sutter

MONTÉE DES ESSES

RUE DE

BOULEVARD DE LA

RUE DE LA TOURETTE

❼

Stade Roger Duplat

RUE DES
CHARTREUX

PLACE DU LT MOREL

RUE PIERRE

RUE DUPONT

Église St-Bruno

RUE ORNANO

RUE

RIVET

COURS

GENÉRAL

GIRAUD

RUE DE

Jardin des Chartreux

QUAI SAINT VINCENT

La Saône

Ⓜ ......Metro Stop
✝ ......Cathedral
ⓘ ......Information
Ⓟ ......Police Station
✈ ......Airport
🚉 ......Railway Stn
✚ ......Hospital

SIGHTS & ATTRACTIONS

Amphithéâtre des Trois Gaules (Three Gaules Amphitheatre)

Unearthed in 1954, and probably built in AD 19 for gladiatorial combat, and other violent games, many an early Christian met their death there. Though you can't actually visit the site itself, which has still to be fully excavated, you can look at it from the montée des Carmélites and the rue Sportisse.

Église St-Bruno (Church of St Bruno)

Designed (apart from its 19th-century façade) by local architect Ferdinand Delamonce, this is Lyon's only baroque church. It was built on the site of an old Carthusian monastery in the 18th century. The canopy is by Soufflet, who also designed the dome of the Hôtel Dieu hospital, and several other buildings in Lyon.

TALL ORDER

Once the 'working hill' as opposed to the 'praying hill' (Fourvière), Croix-Rousse developed as it is today in the early 19th century because of the invention of the Jacquard silk loom, which was too big for the buildings in Vieux Lyon. As a result, most of the unadorned tall buildings in Croix-Rousse, with their high windows, sprang up to house silk looms and weavers – who also lived in them. Naturally, today these five-storey buildings, with their lofty oak-beamed interiors (the silk looms were attached to the beams), have been converted into much sought-after apartments.

There are occasional concerts of music suitable to the venue –
check with the tourist office.

ⓐ rue Pierre Dupont (near rue des Chartreux) 🕐 15.00–17.00
Mon–Sat, closed public holidays

Boulevard de la Croix-Rousse

Leading off the Place de la Croix-Rousse is the boulevard de la
Croix-Rousse, with its colourful morning food market (except
Monday). The square and the boulevard are the scene of a
funfair, la Vogue, held in autumn, from October to mid-
November. Roasted chestnuts are a feature of the festivities.
Running north from the boulevard de la Croix-Rousse is another
main street, full of shops, the boulevard des Canuts. Go up here
to the junction of rue Denfert Rochereau and you will find one
of Lyon's best *trompe-l'oeil* painted walls. It is also the largest,
first created in 1987 but repainted in 1997.

🔺 *The houses of Croix-Rousse looking out over Lyon*

Joseph-Marie Jacquard, inventor of the silk loom

Traboules

Croix-Rousse also has many *traboules* (marked by a lion's head symbol) that go north–south, and are used by locals as shortcuts to and from Presqu'île. *Traboule* routes are indicated by arrows next to the lion's head symbols. One of the most interesting leads from the cour des Voraces. The courtyard and its huge stairway, which looks like it's made of concrete but is in fact stone, gets its name from Canuts (see box below) who rebelled in the 19th century. According to legend the Voraces (voracious ones) protested when the size of a pot of wine was reduced from 1 litre to 46 cl – a size still used today throughout

---

SILK WEAVERS

The main square is the place de la Croix-Rousse, in which there is a statue of Joseph-Marie Jacquard, inventor of the loom bearing his name. He designed the machine in the early 19th century. With its perforated card system, it made weaving complex designs much easier, but also led to a cutback in the number of weavers that were needed. As a result, the Canuts (silk weavers) rebelled several times in the early 19th century, because of unemployment and poor wages. Eventually some of the silk workshops moved out of Lyon, and later, silkworm disease, the loss of foreign markets and the development of synthetic fabrics in the early 20th century, meant that silk weaving gradually disappeared from Lyon almost entirely. Only a few high-quality operations remain, mostly restoring old silk or catering for leading fashion houses.

● *Admire the old silk looms at the Maison des Canuts*

Lyon. There are several ways into the *traboule*: 9 place Colbert (accessible from boulevard de la Croix-Rousse), 14 bis montée St-Sébastien and 29 rue Imbert Colomès. The *traboules* of Lyon generally, but those in Croix-Rousse in particular, were very important to the French Resistance in Lyon during World War II. The movement was led locally by Jean Moulin (he was later tortured by the Germans, before his death in 1943), whose base was in Croix-Rousse.

CULTURE

Maison des Canuts (House of the Silk Weavers)

The 45-minute guided tours at this museum take you through the history of silk and how it was woven on hand looms – with demonstrations – as well as how silk weavers lived. The museum is also an active workshop, restoring old silk. There is a shop across the road (where you buy your ticket) that sells silk scarves, ties and fabrics. Although there are only two guided visits a day, you can always pop into the shop, where old looms are also kept, and ask if you can look at the workshop.

ⓐ 10 rue d'Ivry ⓣ 04 78 28 62 04 ⓦ www.maisondescanuts.com
ⓛ 10.00–18.30 Tues–Sat, guided tours 11.00 and 15.30, closed public holidays & first week in Jan. Admission charge

RETAIL THERAPY

As a residential area, Croix-Rousse doesn't have much more to drain your wallet or handbag than everyday shops. But there is a food market, with over 100 stallholders on the boulevard de la

◗ *Designer shops lined up along passage Thiaffait*

Croix-Rousse from 06.00–12.30 Tues–Sun. You should also try the covered passage Thiaffait, on the slopes of the hill, with fashion and other designer shops. ⓦ www.passagethiaffait.fr. There's also the Maison des Canuts (see page 99).

TAKING A BREAK

Le Canut et les Gones £–££ ❶ A *bouchon* concentrating on fresh, local produce. ⓐ 29 rue de Belfort ⓣ 04 78 29 17 23 ⓒ closed Sun & Mon ⓝ Metro: Croix-Rousse

Le Canut Sans Cervelle £–££ ❷ With a patio, serving traditional cuisine and well known for Sunday brunch from Sept–May. Good value at lunchtime. ⓐ 4 bis rue de Belfort ⓣ 04 78 30 10 20 ⓒ 12.00–14.00, 19.30–22.30, closed Wed & Sat dinner ⓝ Metro: Croix-Rousse

AFTER DARK

Restaurants
Comptoir du Mail £–££ ❸ A favourite with locals, you can get a simple snack or a more intricate dinner. ⓐ 14 rue du Mail ⓣ 04 78 27 71 40 ⓒ 12.00–13.45, 19.00–21.45 Tues–Sat ⓝ Metro: Croix-Rousse

La Famille £–££ ❹ A friendly family-run place, serving generous portions of filling comfort food at decent prices, particularly at lunchtime. ⓐ 18 rue Duviard ⓣ 04 72 98 83 90 ⓒ 12.00–14.00, 19.30–22.30 Tues–Sat ⓝ Metro: Croix-Rousse

Maison Villemanzy £–££ In a house on the slopes of Croix-Rousse, with a terrace offering fine views and tempting food that's cooked to a high standard. 🅐 25 montée St-Sébastien 🅣 04 72 98 21 21 🅛 12.00–14.00, 19.30–22.00, closed Mon lunch, Sun 🅝 Metro: Croix-Paquet

Le Plato £–££ Seasonal market cuisine, with some unusual twists (duck breast with coriander, for instance). Also a very good wine list. 🅐 1 rue Villeneuve 🅣 04 72 00 01 30 🅛 12.00–14.30, 19.30–23.30, closed Sun 🅝 Metro: Croix-Rousse

Entertainment
There isn't much late night activity in Croix-Rousse, but you could try:

Modern Art Café A bar displaying contemporary art, with a DJ in the evening and good cocktails. You can also eat light dishes, and go for brunch (11.00–15.00) on Sundays. You can sit outside in good weather. 🅐 65 bd de la Croix-Rousse 🅣 04 72 87 06 82 🅛 11.30–02.00 summer, 17.00–02.00 winter 🅝 Metro: Croix-Rousse

🅑 *The pretty cloisters of St-André le Bas, Vienne*

Pérouges

The small hill village of Pérouges, built between the 12th and 15th centuries, is officially designated as one of the most beautiful in France, and would make a good half-day trip as a contrast to the bustle of Lyon. The hill was once the site of a Roman watchtower, and legend has it that the village was founded by a tribe of Gauls from Perugia in Italy (hence its name). Whether or not this is true, a castle was built on the hill in the 12th century, and the site was fortified. Pérouges has changed hands many times during its long history. It was once Dauphinois, and in 1345 came under the rule of the Dukes of Savoy. It eventually became French in 1601. It was during its Savoyard period that Pérouges had its finest hour, withstanding a siege by the Dauphinois in 1468. The part of the village that was then outside the fortifications was, however, destroyed, and the inhabitants then moved to the top of the hill, within the ramparts. Pérouges was known as a centre of crafts, in particular the weaving of hemp cloth. It is a charming and peaceful place, with some excellent views, interesting shops and decent restaurants.

GETTING THERE

The best ways of getting to Pérouges, which is 34 km (21 miles) northeast of Lyon, are to take a train from Perrache station to Meximieux (34–49 minutes, depending on the train), and then walk or take a taxi; or drive via the A6/E15 and the Périphérique, following signs to Genève. Leave the motorway at exit 6, and reach Pérouges via La Valbonne and Meximieux (around 45 minutes altogether). You can park by the church. ❶ Make sure you take comfortable walking shoes, as the streets are all pebbled.

SIGHTS & ATTRACTIONS

The main attraction of Pérouges is simply wandering around the village itself. You enter through a gateway, the Porte d'en Haut (the Upper Gate, the only remaining part of the 12th-century castle), past the remnant of a 15th-century gate. The tourist office (Syndicat d'Initiative) is located at the entrance to the village. ❶ 04 74 61 01 14 Ⓦ www.perouges.org

PERFECT PÉROUGES

Its perfect look today (apart from the odd car, there are few visible signs of modernity) belies the fact that it was semi-derelict at the beginning of the 20th century. It had only a handful of inhabitants and was in danger of being demolished. Though today it still has only 73 full-time inhabitants for its 200 houses, it has undergone steady and careful restoration since 1911. The village is built almost entirely of pebbles (from the local rivers) and bricks, as stone was in short supply, and was only used to support doors, windows and the corners of houses. The success of its restoration has meant not only that it attracts many visitors, particularly during the summer, but that it has often been used as a period location for TV and films, including *The Three Musketeers*.

Lyon region

0   10 km
0   6 miles

Villefranche-sur-Saône

Saône

A46

Tarare

A6

L'Arbresle

RHÔNE

Villeurbanne

Feurs

LYON

Ste-Foy-l'Argentière

Oullins

Loire

Brignais

Montrond-les-Bains

A72

Givors

A7

A46

LOIRE

A47

Vienne

Rive-de-Gier

St-Étienne

Roche-la-Molière

St-Maurice-l'Exil

Firminy

Rhône

Loire

Bourg-Argental

HAUTE-LOIRE

Annonay

A7

St-Vallier

ARDÈCHE

○ ....City
○ ....Large Town
○ ....Small Town
▬ ....Motorway
— ....Main Road
— ....Minor Road
✈ ....Airport
▬ ....Railway

N

◐ *A cluster of rooftops in the beautiful village of Pérouges*

Église St-Marie-Madeleine (Church of St Mary Magdalene)

The simple and peaceful 15th-century church next to the gate is the Église St-Marie-Madeleine. It once formed part of the village's fortifications.

Place du Tilleul

You should eventually reach the attractive main square, place du Tilleul (also known as place de la Halle since it once housed the covered market). The lime tree, known as the 'Tree of Liberty', in the middle of the square was planted in 1792 during the French Revolution. Running around the place du Tilleul is the circular rue des Rondes, from which all streets eventually lead to the main square. Walk along the rue des Rondes and you will reach the Porte d'en Bas (Lower Gate) with its inscription commemorating the siege of 1468. There is a music festival in the village from mid-May–mid-June, and a Christmas market in the place du Tilleul.

CULTURE

Musée du Vieux Pérouges (Museum of Old Pérouges)

Overseen by the Ostellerie (see page 112), the museum is a late 14th- and early 15th-century building, once belonging to the Dukes of Savoy who used it as a hunting lodge. There is a great view of the surrounding area from the tower. You can also visit the mock-medieval garden, which was designed in the 1960s in period style. The museum contains a couple of old looms, photographs of the restoration of the village, and a few pieces of old furniture. Unfortunately, some of the best furniture was

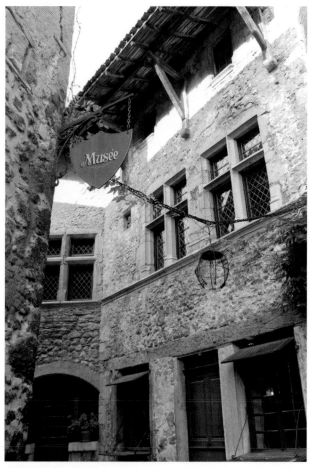

The Musée du Vieux Pérouges

stolen a few years ago. @ rue des Princes ① 04 74 61 00 88
🕐 10.00–12.00, 14.00–16.00 Easter–Sept, and weekends in Oct.
Admission charge

RETAIL THERAPY

Pérouges doesn't offer any exciting shopping experiences, but
there are a few pleasant shops, mostly offering an eclectic range
of goods and souvenirs. They are all in the place du Tilleul or the
rue des Rondes – neither of which has street numbers.

Boulangerie (Didier Rapaud) An artisanal bakery with an old
oven. Sells bread and galettes. @ rue des Rondes ① 04 74 61 39 81
🕐 05.00–20.00, closed Tues Easter–Sept and Mon Oct–Easter

Caveau St-Vincent This local wine shop sells pottery, jams,
carafes and glasses as well as wine, including the sweet
medieval-style Hypocras. You can also have a drink and some
charcuterie downstairs. @ rue des Rondes ① 04 74 61 19 39
🕐 09.30–19.00 May–mid-Nov; 09.30–13.00, 14.30–19.00 Sat &
Sun, mid-Nov–Apr

Cellier de l'Ostellerie Sells glass, pottery, jams, wine and other
items. @ pl du Tilleul ① 04 74 61 08 45 🕐 09.00–12.00, 13.30–18.30

Christine Usdin This foundry, opposite the bakery, has an
interesting range of cast objects by Christine Usdin, the only
foundrywoman in France. Items can be made to order. @ rue des
Rondes ⓦ www.christineusdin.fr.tc 🕐 10.00–19.00

L'Estanco Difficult to define: a tobacconist also selling souvenirs, swords, shields, 'medieval' clothing, wine and beer. rue des Rondes 04 74 61 07 20 Mon–Sun Easter–Oct; Sat & Sun Nov–Easter

TAKING A BREAK

Le Relais de la Tour £ You walk in to be greeted by a suit of armour. You can get drinks, ice cream, *galettes*, salads or fuller meals (only served 12.00–15.00). Enter into the spirit and try some Hypocras medieval-style wine. There are tables on the square in summer. pl du Tilleul 04 74 61 01 03

AFTER DARK

Bars & restaurants
Note that restaurant opening varies considerably according to the season. But most are open at weekends.

Auberge du Coq £ Regional cuisine, pizzas and excellent *galettes* (normally washed down with cider). rue des Rondes 04 74 61 05 47

Le Veneur Noir £–££ A bar and restaurant with a terrace. Specialises in meat cooked on hot stones. at the entrance of the village 04 74 61 07 06

Ostellerie du Vieux Pérouges ££–£££ There has been an inn on this site since the 14th century, though the present building

◯ *Dine at the charming Ostellerie du Vieux Pérouges*

dates from the 18th century, and was restored in 1912. The price symbol applies to the restaurant: the Ostellerie also has a more casual tearoom for snacks. The restaurant draws people from around the area for its excellent local cuisine and fish. It even attracted Bill Clinton in 1996. The waitresses wear white caps and pinafores, and the wine list is written on parchment. ⓐ pl du Tilleul ❶ 04 74 61 00 88

ACCOMMODATION

If you want to stay in medieval Pérouges itself, the options are:

Casa la Signora di Perugia ££–£££ Stylish, if expensive chambre d'hôte, with a terrace and two small pools. The five suites are all decorated according to historical themes. ⓐ Porte d'en Bas ❶ 04 74 61 47 03 ⓦ www.casaperugia.com

Ostellerie de Pérouges ££–£££ Rates vary depending on whether you stay in the main building (more expensive) or another one on the main square. The hotel has 28 comfortable rooms. ⓐ pl du Tilleul ❶ 04 74 61 00 88 ⓦ www.ostellerie.com

Vienne

Designated one of the 120 'Towns of Art and History' by France's Ministry of Culture, you'll see why once you start walking around Vienne's historic centre. The narrow streets, pleasant squares and a mixture of architecture – from the Roman period onwards – are barely matched by other French towns of its size. A day trip is easily enough to squeeze in all the main sights.

Vienne has been inhabited since the 3rd century BC (originally by a group of Gauls called the Allobroges) and became a Roman colony in around AD 40. The town developed along both banks of the Rhône and became one of the largest settlements in Gaul. Evidence of its importance in Roman times is visible throughout the town today. Vienne later became an important centre of Christianity, coming under the rule of the Burgundians in the late 5th century. In the 11th century, the town became part of the Holy Roman Empire, and then part of the kingdom of France in 1450. But its fortunes declined as it was gradually overshadowed by Lyon.

There was an economic revival in the late 18th century, thanks to the establishment of textile factories and metallurgical works along the River Gère, to the north of the old town, and the population grew as a result. However, by the mid-20th century, the textile industry had largely disappeared in the face of competition. Today, Vienne, with a population of 30,000, is the home of service businesses, with some hi-tech industries. Two bridges, one a footbridge, cross over to the west bank of the Rhône.

GETTING THERE

It's easy to get to Vienne from Lyon by train (from either Perrache or Part-Dieu stations) – the journey time is 20–30 minutes. The train station is next to the old town. If you want to drive from Lyon, take the A7, following signs to Marseille and then to Vienne itself. It should take 30–35 minutes.

SIGHTS & ATTRACTIONS

Head down either the rue Boson or the attractive cours Romestang (both come off the cours Brillier) to get into the heart of the old town. If you go down the rue Boson, you will go past the church of St-Pierre and its archaeological museum. Both rue Boson and cours Romestang will also lead you to the Cathédrale St-Maurice and – to the east of it – the place de Miremont, which houses the Musée des Beaux-Arts et d'Archéologie (see page 121). A little farther north, and you will get to the place Charles de Gaulle, and the temple of the former Roman forum. There are cafés outside the temple, from which you can admire it. The tower you will see to the right was once part of a palace, and dates from the 16th century. Heading down the pedestrianised rue des Clercs, you will reach the church of St-André le Bas (see page 119), with its immensely attractive cloisters, which overlooks the Rhône.

You should also try to find time to cross the Rhône to have a look at the museum and site of St-Romain-en-Gaul. And, if you can, take the ten-minute walk along the cours de Verdun, south from the cours Brillier (which has a small park coming off it near

⬣ *You can't miss Vienne's Roman Pyramide*

the tourist office) and take a look at Vienne's famous Pyramide, once the centrepiece of the Roman circus, where chariot races took place. You might also be tempted to have a drink at the Pyramide hotel (see pages 125 and 126), one of France's most famous temples of gastronomy.

At the start of your visit, you can get an audio guide from the tourist office and follow the path marked by plaques on the ground. You can also get a combined museum ticket costing €6.

Cathédrale St-Maurice

The dark and imposing cathedral (a parish church since 1790) was built between the late 11th and the early 16th centuries. The exterior, which is being slowly restored, is Gothic though the interior is a mixture of Romanesque and Gothic styles. There had been an earlier cathedral on the site since the 4th or 5th century. There are carvings of biblical scenes throughout, and intriguing zodiac carvings in the choir. Some of the masonry used in the cathedral's construction is actually Roman in origin.
ⓐ pl St-Paul ❶ 04 74 85 60 28 ◷ 08.30–18.00

JAZZ IT UP

The main event in Vienne is its well-known jazz festival (Jazz à Vienne), which takes place from late June–mid-July around town, but particularly in the Roman theatre (see page 122). Details and tickets are available from the tourist office. There is also a fête in mid-June. Tourist office:
ⓐ cours Brillier (just by the Rhône) ❶ 04 74 53 80 30
ⓦ www.vienne-tourisme.com

Église & Cloître St-André le Bas (Church & Cloister of St-André le Bas)

Once part of an important abbey founded in the 6th century, the church was substantially rebuilt in the 11th and 12th centuries. It is notable for its Romanesque ornamentation. Unfortunately, you can't visit it without a guide. You can, however, visit the very pleasing 12th-century cloister, in which several of the pillars are differently decorated. The building adjoining the cloister houses temporary art exhibitions.

ⓐ pl du Jeu-de-Paume ⓣ 04 74 85 18 49 ⓛ 09.30–13.00, 14.00–18.00 Tues–Sun, Apr–Oct; 09.30–12.30, 14.00–17.00 Tues–Fri, 14.00–18.00 Sat & Sun, Nov–Mar. Admission charge

⬤ *The striking interior of the Cathédrale St-Maurice*

Jardin Archéologique de Cybèle (Archaeological Garden)

These Roman ruins, now essentially a park, as well as a venue during the Jazz Festival (see page 118), were properly excavated when the hospital standing on the site was knocked down. One side of the site formed part of the forum, and is thought to have contained baths and a small theatre or odeon. It is also a good place to have a picnic. Nearby is the place du Pilori, where you will find a timber-framed medieval house.

ⓐ rue des Orfèvres

Temple d'Auguste & de Livie (Temple of Augustus & Livia)

Originally built around 20–10 BC, the temple (the centre of the Roman forum) was dedicated to Roman emperors, Augustus in particular, during whose reign it was constructed. In the early Middle Ages (probably 6th century) it became a church with walls between the columns – a fact that helped to preserve it. It was restored in the late 19th century. You can't actually enter it without a guide (book through the tourist office).

ⓐ pl Charles de Gaulle

CULTURE

Musée Archéologique & Église St-Pierre (Archaeological Museum & Church of St Pierre)

Dating from the 5th or 6th century, this church is one of the oldest in France, configured as a basilica. The belfry was built in the 12th century. It has housed an archaeological museum since 1872, which includes ancient Gallo-Roman sculptures, masonry and mosaics.

ⓐ pl St-Pierre ⓣ 04 74 85 20 35 ⓛ 09.30–13.00, 14.00–18.00
Tues–Sun, Apr–Oct; 09.30–12.30, 14.00–17.00 Tues–Fri,
14.00–18.00 Sat & Sun, Nov–Mar. Admission charge

Musée des Beaux-Arts & d'Archéologie (Fine Arts & Archaeological Museum)

Rather old-fashioned, and not the most inspiring museum you
will come across, but the first floor houses a collection of local
Gallic and Gallo-Roman artefacts (including some fine
silverware), as well as 18th-century earthenware and 16th- to
19th-century works by local artists. The building, a former grain
market, was built in the early 19th century, and is set in the
centre of the square. Temporary exhibitions, and events such as
arts and craft fairs, as well as a Christmas market, are held on
the ground floor.

ⓐ pl de Miremont ⓣ 04 74 85 50 42 ⓛ 09.30–13.00, 14.00–18.00
Tues–Sun, Apr–Oct; 09.30–12.30, 14.00–17.00 Tues–Fri,
14.00–18.00 Sat & Sun, Nov–Mar. Admission charge

Musée de Saint-Romain-en-Gal

On the west bank of the Rhône just beyond the road bridge, the
archaeological site was a district of Roman Vienne, dating from
the 1st century AD, and full of workshops, shops and warehouses
in ancient times. The 7-hectare (17-acre) site began to be
excavated in the late 1960s. You can wander around it, and get
some idea of how the Romans lived. It also has two picnic areas.
The ultra-modern steel and glass museum – from which you
can see the site – opened in 1996. The well-laid-out displays and
models, including murals and some stunning mosaics, are

designed to illustrate Roman daily life. There are great views of the Rhône and Vienne, particularly from the brasserie, closed at the time of writing, but due to reopen during 2007.

ⓐ rte départementale 502 ⓣ 04 74 53 74 01 ⓦ www.musees-gallo-romains.com ⓛ 10.00–18.00 Tues–Sun. Admission charge

Théâtre Romain (Roman Theatre)

Likely to have been built in around AD 40–50 into the side of a hill, this is one of the largest theatres of the Roman world. It is 130 m (426 ft) in diameter, and was once capable of holding

🔺 *The Théâtre Romain is now a music concert venue*

13,000 spectators. Excavation and restoration took from 1923–38. It is now the main venue for the Jazz Festival (see page 118), as well as being used for rock concerts and other musical events. If you enjoy a degree of comfort, take a cushion.
ⓐ rue du Cirque ① 04 74 85 39 23 ① 09.30–13.00, 14.00–18.00 Apr–Aug; 09.30–13.00, 14.00–18.00 Tues–Sun, Sept–Oct; 09.30–12.00, 14.00–17.00 Tues–Fri, 13.30–17.30 Sat & Sun, Nov–Mar. Admission charge

RETAIL THERAPY

There are several interesting shops near the main sights, particularly in rue des Clercs, the rue Joseph Brenier and rue Marchande. You will also find plenty of shops, including chain stores, pharmacies and banks around the place de Miremont. There is an excellent market in place François Mitterand on weekday mornings, but nothing to rival the huge market – one of the biggest in France – that covers much of the old town on Saturday mornings.

Boutique Patrick Henriroux The shop of the Pyramide hotel and restaurant (see pages 125 and 126) sells wine, kitchen equipment, spices, sauces, mustards, crockery and other culinary items. ⓐ 14 bd Fernand Point ① 04 74 53 01 96

Carréblanc Part of the French chain selling brightly coloured and interestingly patterned bed linen, bathrobes, towels and other household items. ⓐ 26 rue Joseph Brenier ① 04 74 31 70 98 ① closed Sun & Mon

Le Cellier One of Vienne's best wine shops, with a very good selection of local wines from the Rhône Valley. ⓐ 50 rue Joseph Brenier ⓣ 04 74 85 40 81 ⓛ closed Sun & Mon.

La Gâterie One of the few traditional pâtisseries left in Vienne, it produces delicious pastries, cakes, biscuits and confectionery. ⓐ 22 rue Juiverie ⓣ 04 74 85 32 59 ⓛ closed Sun & Mon

Natalys Fun and high quality children's clothing. ⓐ 69 rue Marchande ⓣ 04 74 78 18 57 ⓛ closed Sun & Mon

Sia Candles, glass and decorative household objects. ⓐ 25 rue Joseph Brenier ⓣ 04 74 85 18 94 ⓛ closed Sun & Mon

TAKING A BREAK

Le Café des Orfèvres £ Straightforward traditional food, renowned for its big salads. ⓐ 31 rue des Orfèvres ⓣ 04 74 31 97 70 ⓛ closed Sun except during the Jazz Festival (see page 118).

La Verre en l'Air £ For drinks and simple meals. ⓐ 14 rue Henry Jacquier ⓣ 04 74 78 01 43 ⓛ closed Sat lunch, Sun dinner & Mon

AFTER DARK

Restaurants
La Chamade £–££ Right in the heart of the old town, a small and simple place with white walls, serving traditional dishes such as snails and *andouillette* (local sausage) at reasonable prices.

🅐 24 rue de Juiverie 🕐 04 74 85 30 34 🕒 closed Sun, Tues dinner & Mon

Ma Grand-Mère £–££ Salads, Lyonnais specialities and very good steaks. 🅐 8 rue du Musée 🕐 04 74 31 61 84

Le Bec Fin ££ Near the cathedral, serving high quality local specialities as well as dishes from other parts of France. 🅐 7 pl St-Maurice 🕐 04 74 85 76 72 🕒 closed Sun, Wed dinner & Mon

Le Cloître ££ One of Vienne's best restaurants. Set on two floors. 🅐 2 rue des Cloîtres 🕐 04 74 31 93 57 Ⓦ www.le-cloitre.net 🕒 closed Sun & public holidays

La Pyramide £££ Founded by the legendary Fernand Point, this is one of the most famous restaurants in France. The food is superb – imaginative, light and modern, with intense flavours. And the owner and chef, Patrick Henriroux, actually cooks there (unusual these days) and personally goes to the market (see page 123) every morning to choose his produce. The prices of the set menus are very good value for the quality, though they're steep if you choose from the à la carte menu. Local wines are sensibly priced. There's a children's menu, and the service is friendly and efficient. Many locals go there. You can eat in the pretty garden in summer. 🅐 14 bd Fernand Point 🕐 04 74 53 01 96 🕒 closed Sun & Mon

Bars

Bar du Temple £ Right in front of the Roman temple, this bar is a popular and friendly meeting place. Outdoor seating in summer. ⓐ 5 pl Charles de Gaulle ⓣ 04 74 31 94 19 ⓛ until 24.00 in summer, closed Sun in winter

Pub 38 £ A lively bar with a pool table. Serves beer, cocktails and ice creams (other snacks are also available). Good for a late drink. ⓐ 5 rue Voltaire ⓣ 04 37 02 08 74 ⓛ closed Sun

ACCOMMODATION

Le Central £ Simple and old-fashioned, but a good, comfortable choice in the old town. ⓐ 7 rue de l'Archevêché ⓣ 04 74 85 18 38 ⓦ www.hotel-central-vienne.com

Hôtel de la Poste £ Basic, but a good budget choice. Located in the old town. ⓐ 47 cours Romestang ⓣ 04 74 95 02 04 ⓦ www.hotel-vienne.fr

La Pyramide £££ *The* hotel in Vienne – and one of the best in the area – famous now for decades, with a guest list including the Duke and Duchess of Windsor, Clark Gable and Rita Hayworth (to name but a few). Stars of the jazz festival (see page 118) also stay there. The rooms are extremely well appointed, and the buffet breakfasts unusual and memorable. ⓐ 14 bd Fernand Point ⓣ 04 74 53 01 96 ⓦ www.lapyramide.com

---

▶ *Lyon street signs*

PRACTICAL
information

Directory

GETTING THERE

By air

British Airways fly direct from the UK to Lyon, with regular flights from Heathrow, Birmingham and Manchester. EasyJet also flies there, from Stansted. Flights can often be very reasonably priced if you book well in advance. Other airlines, including Air France, fly there indirectly, but these flights take much longer. Flying British Airways from Heathrow takes around 1 hour and 45 minutes.

British Airways ☎ 0870 850 9 850 ⓦ www.ba.com

easyJet ☎ 0871 244 2366 ⓦ www.easyjet.com

Lyon St-Exupéry International Airport ☎ 04 72 22 72 21 ⓦ www.lyonairport.com

Many people are aware that air travel emits CO_2, which contributes to climate change. You may be interested in the possibility of lessening the environmental impact of your flight through the charity Climate Care, which offsets your CO_2 by funding environmental projects around the world. Visit ⓦ www.climatecare.org

By train

From London (Waterloo at the time of writing, but St Pancras from November 2007) you can get to Lyon by Eurostar, changing for a TGV at either Paris – where you have to transfer from the Gare du Nord to the Gare de Lyon – or Lille. Trains going via Lille stop at Lyon Part-Dieu station, and usually have a slightly shorter journey time since you will need to allow around an hour to transfer between the two Paris stations. Some trains from Paris also stop at Lyon Perrache station. The total journey time via Paris is just under 6 hours.

Eurostar reservations (UK) ☎ 08705 186 186
🌐 www.eurostar.com
French Railways (SNCF) 🌐 www.sncf.com
Rail Europe ☎ 08705 848 848 🌐 www.raileurope.co.uk

By road

There are several routes you can take to get to Lyon from Calais. Either you can take the A26, the A1 and A3 and go via the outskirts of Paris, ending up on the A6, or you can skirt around Paris, and eventually join the A6 further south. Remember to have euros or a credit card with you to pay for toll roads. The distance from Calais is around 750 km (465 miles), and it should take you 6–7 hours.

⬤ *International flights arrive at the modern St-Exupéry airport*

The driving time from Paris is around 4 hours. The quickest way to cross the Channel with a car is by Eurotunnel, although there are also several ferry companies depending on which port you start your journey from.

Eurotunnel ☎ 08705 35 35 35 ⓦ www.eurotunnel.com

For route map: ⓦ www.rac.co.uk

ENTRY FORMALITIES
Documentation

Passports are needed by UK visitors and all others except EU citizens who can produce a national identity card. Visits of up to three months do not require a visa if your nationality is US, Canadian, Australian or New Zealand. Other travellers should consult the French embassy, consulate or tourist office in their own country about visa requirements. ⓦ www.diplomatie.gouv.fr

Customs

Residents of the UK, Ireland and other EU countries may bring into France personal possessions and goods for personal use, including a reasonable amount of tobacco and alcohol, provided they have been bought in the EU. There are few formalities at the points of entry into France. Residents of non-EU countries, and EU residents arriving from a non-EU country, may bring in up to 400 cigarettes and 50 cigars or 50 g (2 oz) tobacco; 2 litres (3 bottles) of wine and 1 litre (approx. 2 pints) of spirits and liqueurs.

MONEY
Currency

The euro (€) is the official currency in France. €1 = 100 cents. It comes in notes of €5, €10, €20, €50, €100, €200 and €500. Coins are in denominations of €1 and €2, and 1, 2, 5, 10, 20 and 50 cents.

Cash machines
ATM machines can be found at St-Exupéry airport and Lyon's railway stations, and are widely available around the city. They accept most British and international debit and credit cards. They are the quickest and most convenient way (and often the cheapest) to obtain cash. Instructions are usually available in English and other major European languages.

Credit cards
Credit cards are almost universally accepted except occasionally at smaller shops, cafés and markets. You will have to know your PIN number, as the chip-and-PIN system is normally used in France. Note that some shops and other establishments have a minimum spend policy, so won't accept cards below a certain limit. VISA is the most frequently accepted card.

Changing currency
You will have no difficulty in finding banks and bureaux de change.

HEALTH, SAFETY & CRIME
It is safe to drink tap water, as most people do, although some prefer to drink mineral water. There are no major precautions you need to take when eating local food and, on the whole, you need worry no more than at home.

Medical care in France is of a very high standard, but expensive unless you have suitable travel insurance. Most minor ailments can be dealt with at pharmacies – of which there are many – indicated by green cross signs. The staff are qualified to offer medical advice and dispense a wide range of medicines.

Lyon is generally safe, but as in all large cities, you should be careful late at night. Otherwise, you should take sensible precautions – particularly in crowded places or at tables outside in restaurants – such as keeping your bag or camera close to you.

In general, the police try to be helpful, but may not speak English. There are three main types of police: the Police Municipale are the ones you are most likely to see overseeing traffic and petty crime, including lost property, in towns; the Police Nationale deal with more serious matters in larger towns; while in country districts and on motorways, the Gendarmerie Nationale, a military force, is the main law enforcement body.

If you are robbed, you should make a statement at your nearest police station to make an insurance claim.

TRAVEL INSURANCE

Visitors from the UK are covered by EU reciprocal health schemes while in France. They require a European Health Insurance Card (EHIC). This will not cover all possible expenses, and only guarantees emergency treatment. You can apply for this online from the UK Department of Health (W www.dh.gov.uk). Always make sure you have adequate travel insurance, covering not only health, but possessions and baggage, etc. All non-EU travellers should make sure they have adequate insurance before they travel.

OPENING HOURS

Shops open 09.00 or 10.00–19.00 or 19.30 Mon–Sat, though some smaller shops open 09.00–12.00, 14.00–19.00. But most shops in tourist areas (such as Vieux Lyon) are normally open all day, and on Sun, and close later; and bakeries, for instance, open earlier. Some shops close on Mon.

Markets usually open at 08.00 or 09.00 (sometimes earlier for food markets) and start packing up around 12.30. Antique, clothes and bric-a-brac markets often close later.

Office hours are usually 08.30–12.00, 14.00–18.00 Mon–Fri. They also close on public holidays.

Banks open 08.30–12.00, 13.30–17.00 Mon–Fri, though times may vary slightly, with some banks open all day, for instance, and others opening later or closing earlier. They are closed on public holidays, and close earlier the day before. So your best bet is to get there mid-morning.

Museums and attractions opening times vary, but they are normally open 10.00– 18.00 or 19.00 in summer. However, some (usually smaller museums) close for lunch, and most have shorter hours outside the high season. Some also close on public holidays, and on either Mon or Tues. Entrance to bigger museums sometimes ends 30 minutes before closing, so always check before you head to them.

TOILETS

You should have no difficulty in finding a toilet. Public buildings, such as museums, usually have clean and modern toilets in the publicly accessible areas near the entrance. Many of Lyon's car parks and metro stations also have toilets. But the fastest and easiest solution is to step into a bar or café and have a quick drink there. There are also public toilets (often modern coin-operated cubicles) on the streets. In Presqu'île, you'll find public toilets in place des Jacobins and place Bellecour; in Croix-Rousse, in place Sathonay and boulevard de la Croix-Rousse; and in Vieux Lyon in rue St-Georges. In Fourvière, they are in place de Fourvière. At the airport, train stations, and in many other public toilets, you may have to pay a small fee (normally €0.50).

CHILDREN

Children are generally welcome in France, and Lyon is no exception. The majority of hotels will normally be very helpful if you are travelling with small children. Most restaurants – particularly cafés and brasseries – gladly serve them. Indeed, many simpler places, and some very grand ones, offer children's menus (*menu enfant*). It is perfectly normal to see well-behaved teenagers, although not infants, eating in posh restaurants. There is also plenty of food on sale that will appeal to kids.

Young children might also be amused by Lyon's painted walls, a cruise along the Saône or Rhône, the Fourvière adventure park (see page 67), the Miniatures Museum (see page 70), the Guignol puppet theatre (see page 68) or the free zoo in Parc de la Tête d'Or on the east bank of the Rhône.

ⓐ access from bd de Brotteaux ☎ 04 78 89 02 03
🕐 for zoo 09.30–18.30 mid-Apr–mid-Oct; 09.30–16.30 rest of
year Ⓜ Metro: Masséna

There is also an Aquarium on the west bank of the Saône.
ⓐ 7 rue Stephane Dechant ☎ 04 72 66 65 66 ⓦ www.
aquariumlyon.fr 🕐 10.00–18.00 Ⓝ Buses: 8, 10, 14 and 17 to Bastero

COMMUNICATIONS

Telephones

The telephone code for the area is 04, followed by an 8-digit
number. When calling from anywhere in France (including Lyon),
dial all 10 digits, including the 04. To dial the area from outside
France, dial your own international prefix (00 in most countries)
followed by 33 4, then the 8-digit local code. Calling from France
to abroad: dial 00 for an international connection, followed by
your country code (UK 44, Republic of Ireland 353, USA and
Canada 1, Australia 61, New Zealand 64, South Africa 27) and
then the area code (leaving out the first 0 if there is one) and
the number. Card-operated public phone booths are
everywhere, and you can make international calls from them.
You can buy phonecards (*télécartes*) at *tabacs*
(newsagent/tobacconists sporting a red diamond sign outside),
post offices and some cafés and railway stations. Some public
phones also accept credit cards. Insert the card after lifting the
receiver. You can also make follow-on calls.

Local directory enquiries 12
International operator 00 33 12 + country code
Freephone numbers start with 0800

Post

Post offices can be found throughout the city. Main offices open 08.00–19.00 Mon–Fri, 08.00–12.00 Sat. The biggest one is on place A. Poncet, next to place Bellecour, by the Rhône. Smaller offices open 09.00–19.00 on weekdays (some closing 12.00–14.00), and are closed Sat afternoons. All post offices are closed Sun and on public holidays. You can also buy stamps in *tabacs*. The postal service is efficient, and postcards to the UK and Ireland will normally arrive in 2–3 days, taking a little longer to non-European destinations.

Current rates for sending postcards are Europe €0.50, North America, Australia and New Zealand €0.90.

Internet

As it's a major business and university city, internet access is widespread in Lyon, with internet cafés easily found (check for addresses with your hotel or local tourist office). And all but the simplest hotels provide internet connections.

ELECTRICITY

France runs on 220 V with 2-pin plugs. British appliances will need a simple adaptor, best obtained from UK electrical shops, or at the Eurostar station or airport. You should also be able to find shops in Lyon selling adaptors. US and other equipment designed for 110 V will normally need a transformer.

TRAVELLERS WITH DISABILITIES

Lyon is generally pretty well adapted to those with disabilities. Many metro stations have lifts down to the platforms (train doors are flush with the platforms), and buses and trams also have access, as do many museums, hotels and restaurants. There are also several pedestrianised streets. The only serious problems might arise in Vieux Lyon, and climbing the slopes of Croix-Rousse (though several of the stairs have ramps). There is also special transport available (check with the tourist office). Useful organisations for advice and information include:

Association de Paralysés de France Provides information for the whole of France. ❷ 17 bd Auguste Blanqui, 75013 Paris ☎ 01 40 78 69 00 ⓦ www.apf.asso.fr

RADAR The principal UK forum and pressure group for people with disabilities. ❷ 12 City Forum, 250 City Road, London EC1V 8AF ☎ 020 7250 3222 ⓦ www.radar.org.uk

SATH (Society for Accessible Travel & Hospitality) Advises US-based travellers with disabilities. ❷ 347 Fifth Ave, Suite 610, New York, NY 10016 ☎ 212 447 7284 ⓦ www.sath.org

TOURIST INFORMATION

The city's tourist office is very helpful ❷ Office du Tourisme, pl Bellecour ☎ 04 72 77 69 69 ⓦ www.lyon-france.com ⓛ 10.00–17.30 Mon–Sat, closed public holidays

Other useful websites are:

ⓦ www.lyon.fr (Lyon's official website)

ⓦ www.mairie-lyon.fr (town hall site)

ⓦ www.rhonealpes-tourisme.com (the regional site)

ⓦ www.franceguide.com (the French tourist board site)

Emergencies

Emergency numbers

The following are all free national emergency numbers:

Medical/ambulance (SAMU) 15

Police 17

Fire (Sapeurs-Pompiers) 18

Any emergency service 112. This is also the number that must be used when calling from mobile phones.

Medical services

Lyon is very well supplied by high quality medical services.

Hospitals:

Croix-Rousse Hospital 🅐 103 Grande rue de la Croix-Rousse 🅣 08 20 08 20 69

Edouard Herriot Hospital 🅐 5 pl Arsonval 🅣 04 72 11 78 83

Hôtel Dieu Hospital 🅐 1 pl de l'Hôpital 🅣 08 20 08 20 69

Doctors:

Maisons Médicales de Gardes They will tell you who to visit near your hotel. 🅣 04 72 33 00 33

PASS 🅣 04 78 29 59 14

Médecins du Monde 🅣 04 78 29 59 14

SOS Medecins For emergencies, 24 hours a day, every day. 🅣 04 78 83 51 51

For dental emergencies, call 🅣 04 72 10 01 01

Pharmacies:

Those listed below are open 24 hours a day, every day.

Pharmacie Blanchet 🅐 5 pl des Cordeliers 🅣 04 78 42 12 42

Pharmacie Duquesne 🅐 36 rue Duquesne 🅣 04 78 93 70 96

Police stations:
Croix-Rousse ⓐ 5 pl Sathonay ⓣ 04 78 28 11 87
Presqu'île ⓐ 47 rue de la Charité ⓣ 04 78 42 26 56
Central Police Station On the east bank of the Rhône. ⓐ Hôtel de Police, 40 rue Maurice Berliet ⓣ 04 78 78 40 40

Embassies & consulates
Australian Embassy ⓐ 4 rue Jean Ray, 75015 Paris ⓣ 01 40 59 33 00
Canadian Consulate ⓐ 17 rue Bourgelat, 69002 Lyon
ⓣ 04 72 77 64 07
Irish Embassy ⓐ 4 rue Rude, 75016 Paris ⓣ 01 44 17 67 00
New Zealand Embassy ⓐ 7 rue Léonard da Vinci, 75016 Paris
ⓣ 01 45 01 43 43
South African Embassy ⓐ 59 quai d'Orsay, 75007 Paris
ⓣ 01 53 59 23 23
United Kingdom Consulate ⓐ 24 rue Childebert, 69002 Lyon
ⓣ 04 72 77 81 70
United States Consulate ⓐ 1 quai Jules Courmont, 69002 Lyon
ⓣ 04 78 38 36 88

EMERGENCY PHRASES
Help! Au secours! *Ossercoor!*   **Fire!** Au feu! *Oh fur!*
Stop! Stop! *Stop!*
Call an ambulance/a doctor/the police/the fire service!
Appelez une ambulance/un médecin/la police/les pompiers!
*Ahperleh ewn ahngbewlahngss/ang medesang/lah poleess/
leh pompeeyeh!*

SPOT A CITY IN SECONDS

This great range of pocket city guides will have you in the know in no time. Lightweight and packed with detail on the most important things from shopping and sights to non-stop nightlife, they knock spots off chunkier, clunkier versions. Titles include:

Available from all good bookshops, your local Thomas Cook travel store or browse and buy on-line at www.thomascookpublishing.com

Thomas Cook Publishing

The publishers would like to thank the following individuals and organisations for providing the copyright photographs for this book:

Anwer Bati: all photographs except
Pictures Colour Library: pages 19, 34, 49, 95, 129
World Pictures: pages 9, 59, 64, 90
Nicolas Rigaud for the Visitors' Bureau of Lyon: page 15

Copy editor: Jenni Rainford
Proofreader: Ian Faulkner

Send your thoughts to
books@thomascook.com

- **Found a great bar, club, shop or must-see sight that we don't feature?**

- **Like to tip us off about any information that needs updating?**

- **Want to tell us what you love about this handy little guidebook and more importantly how we can make it even handier?**

Then here's your chance to tell all! Send us ideas, discoveries and recommendations today and then look out for your valuable input in the next edition of this title. As an extra 'thank you' from Thomas Cook Publishing, you'll be automatically entered into our exciting prize draw.

Send an email to the above address (stating the book's title) or write to: CitySpots Project Editor, Thomas Cook Publishing, PO Box 227, The Thomas Cook Business Park, Unit 18, Coningsby Road, Peterborough PE3 8SB, UK.